THIS BOOK BELONGS TO

You May Enjoy Other Books

By Rae Maker

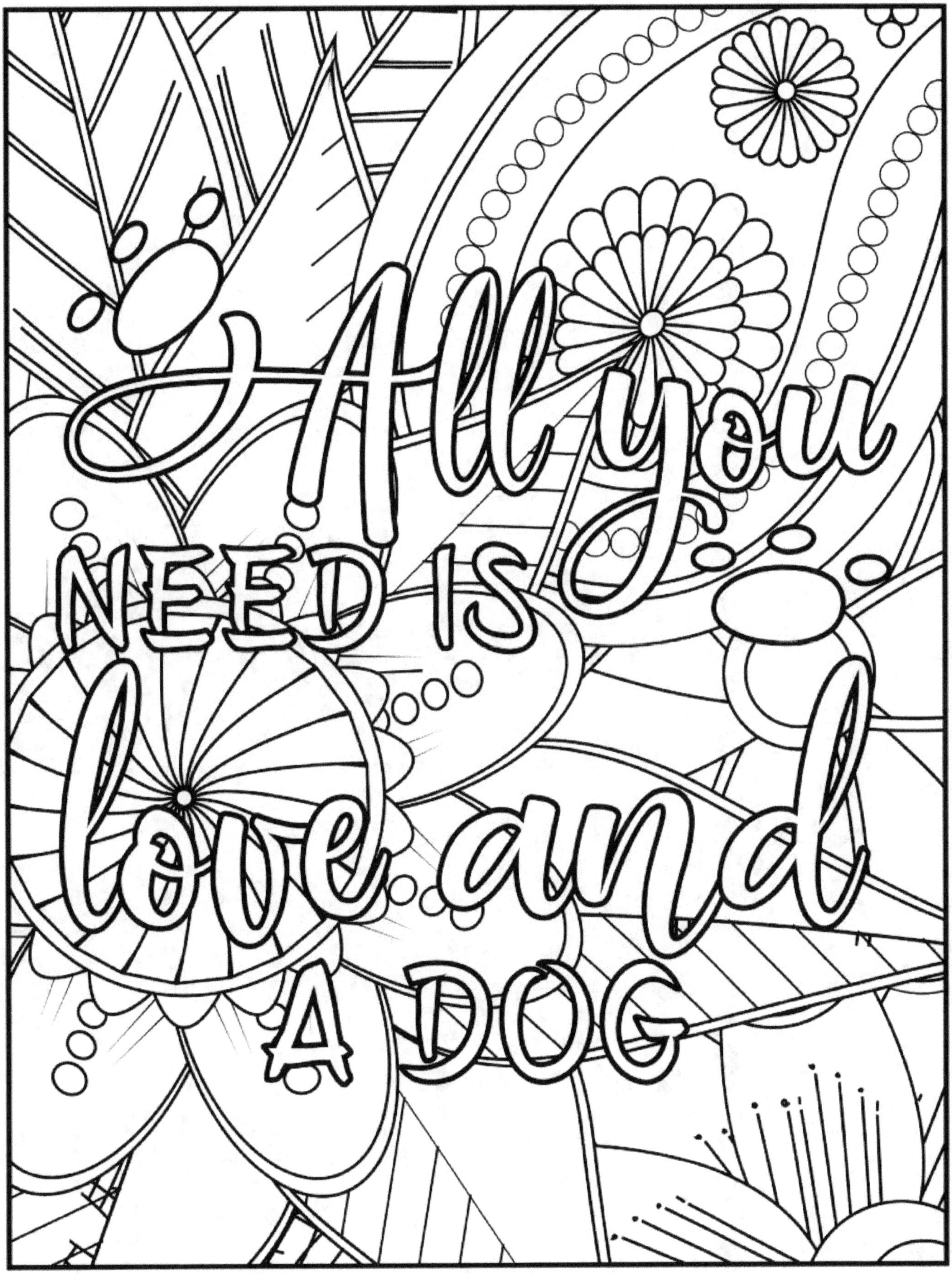
All you
NEED IS
love and
A DOG

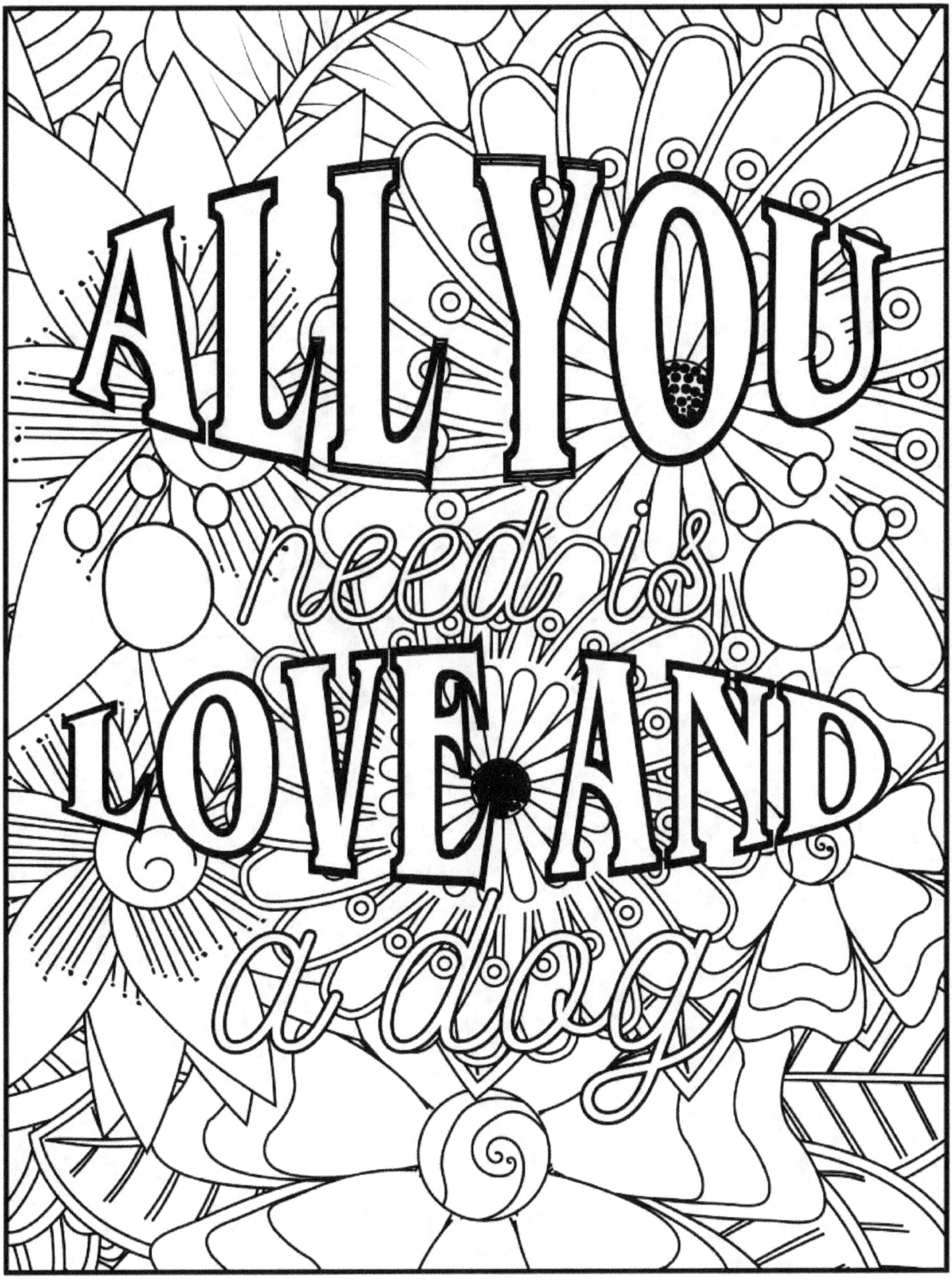
ALL YOU
need is
LOVE AND
a dog

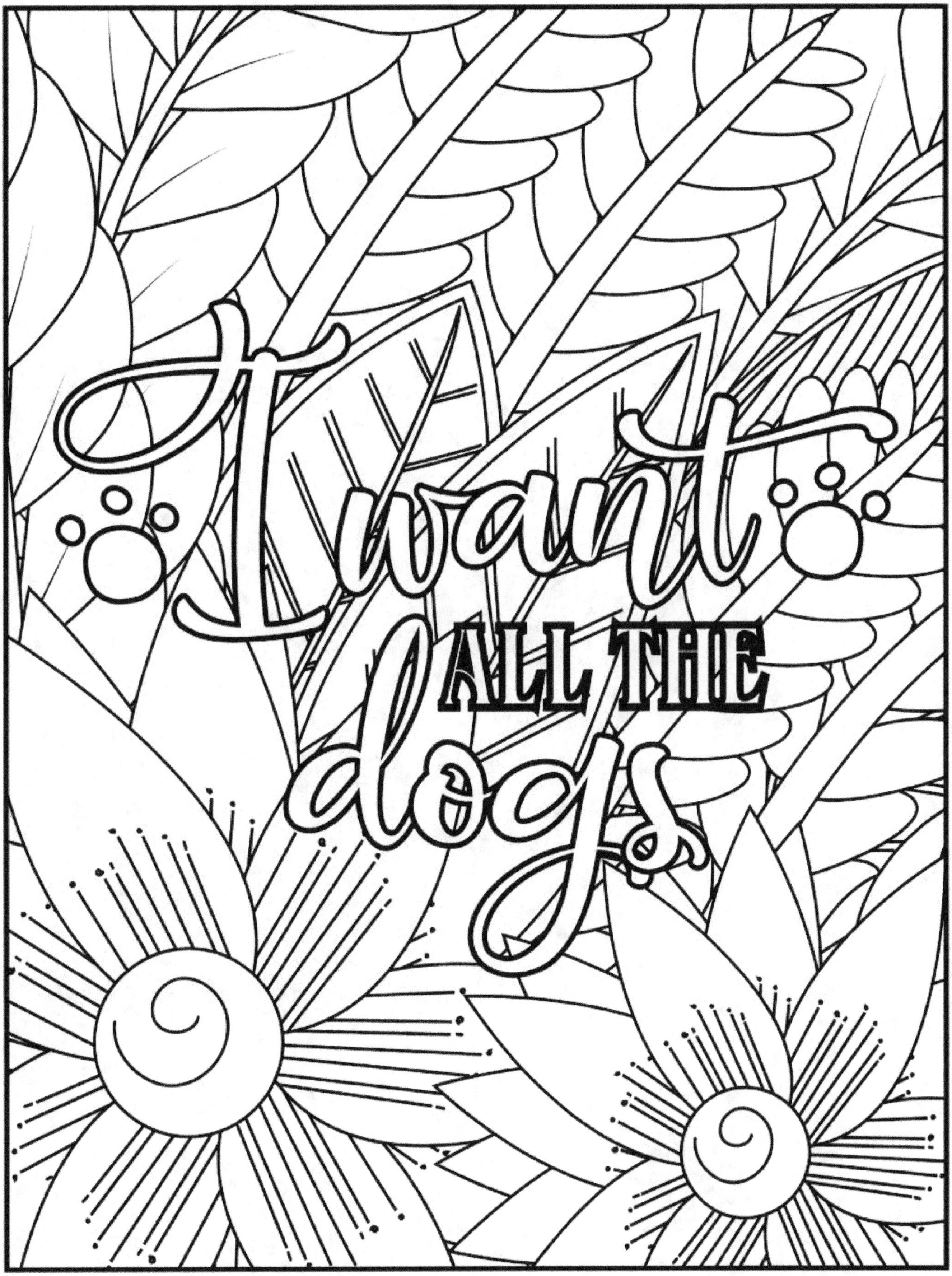
I want
ALL THE
dogs

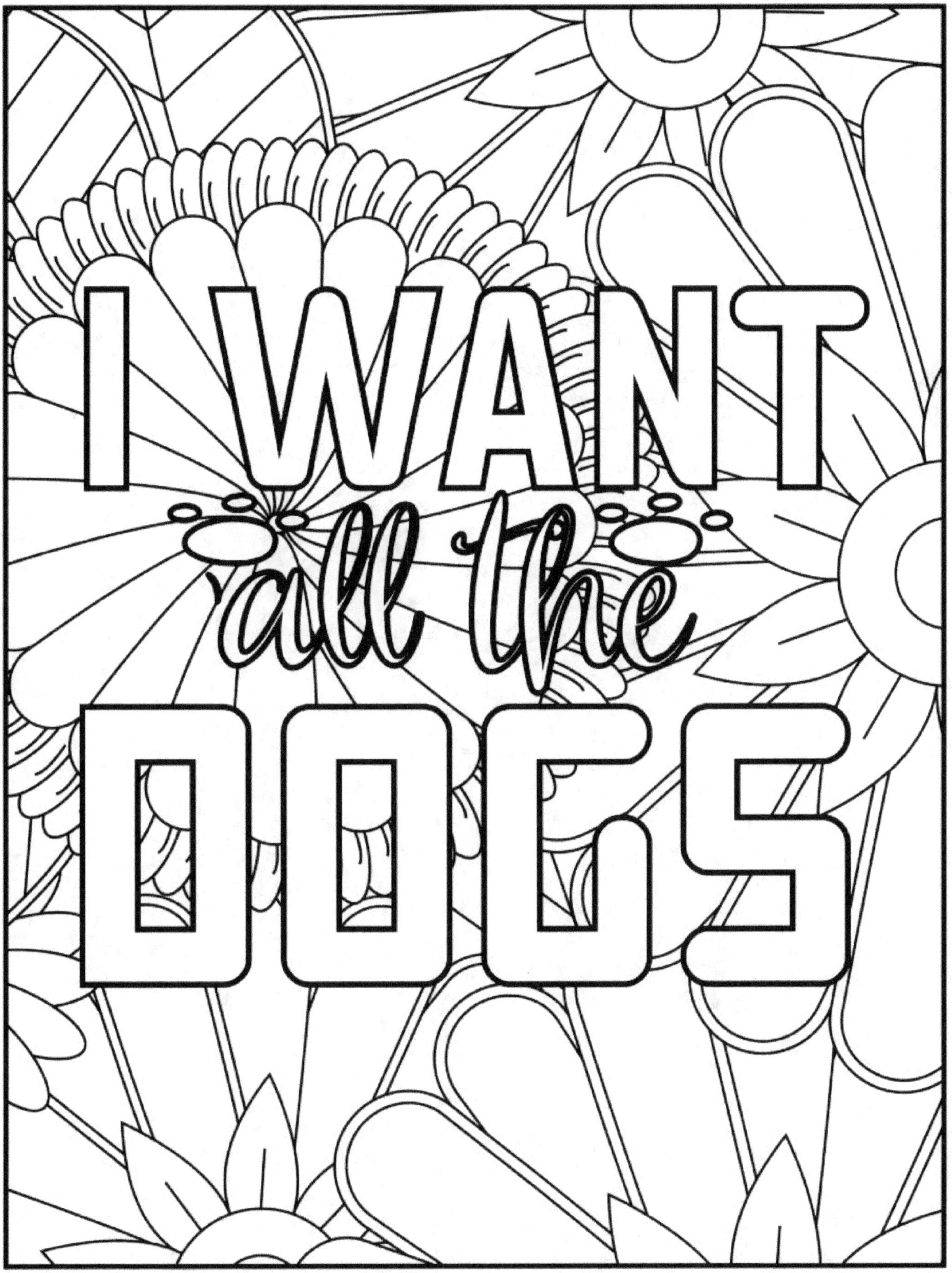
I WANT
all the
DOGS

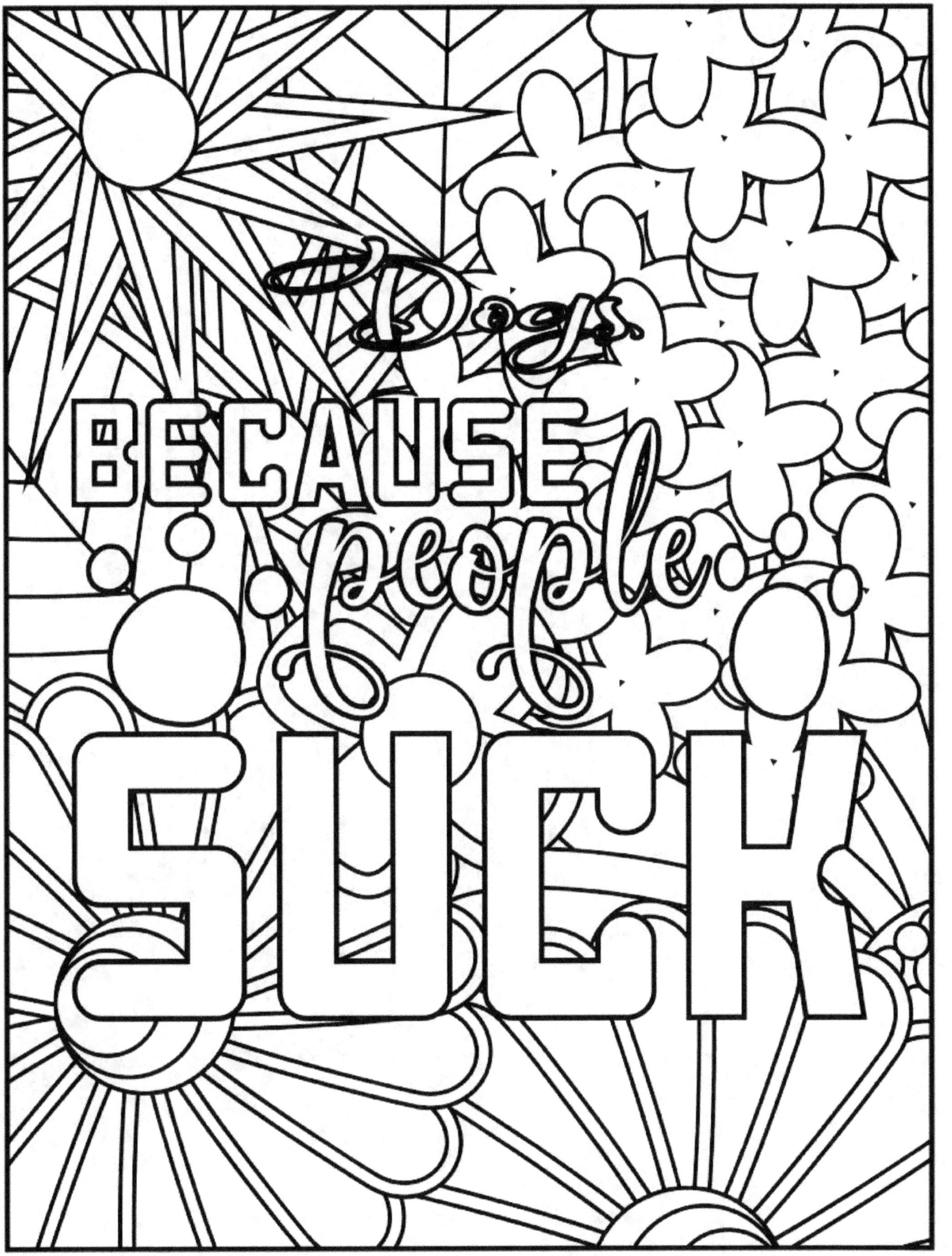
Dogs
BECAUSE people
SUCK

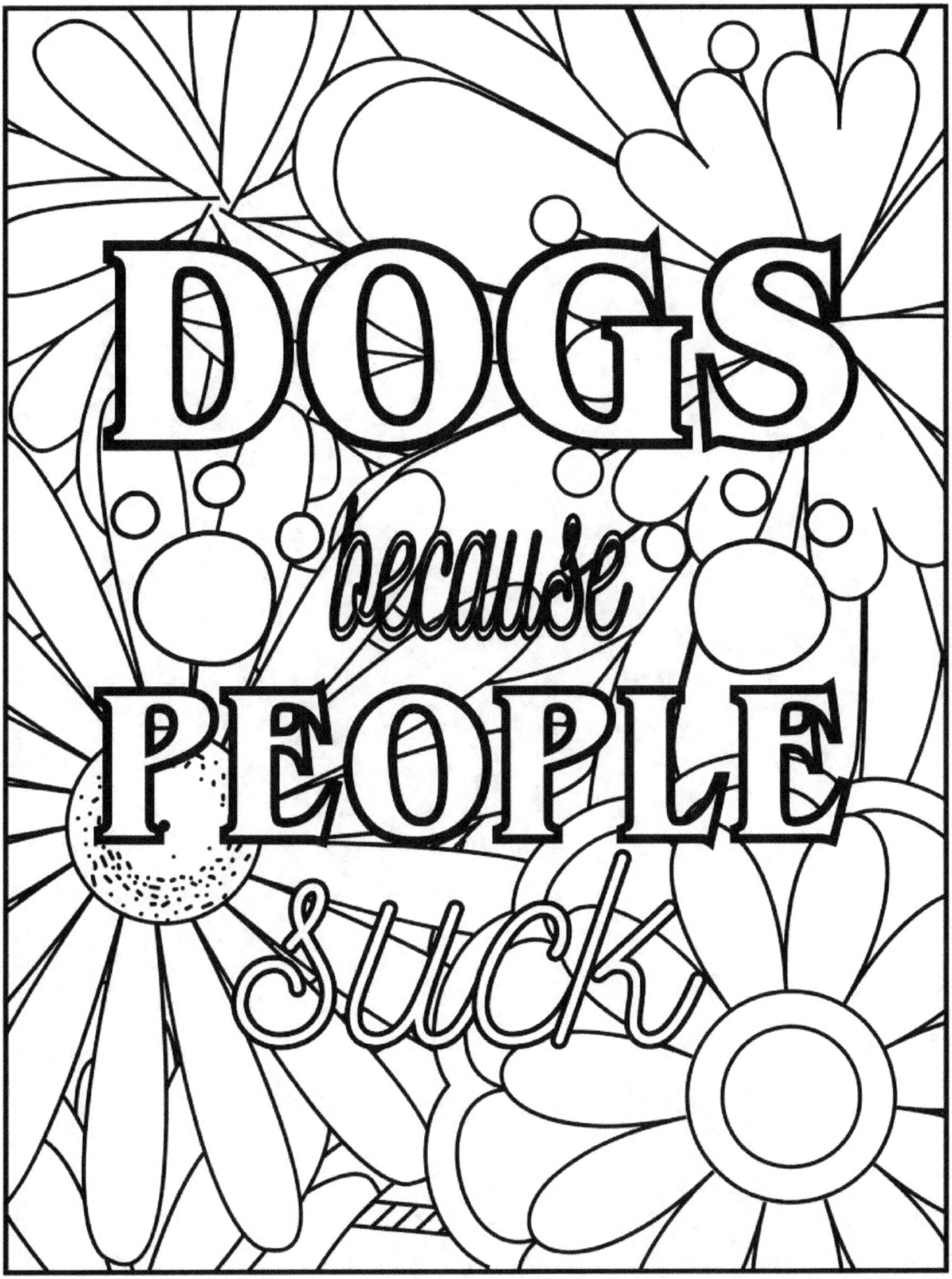
DOGS
because
PEOPLE
suck

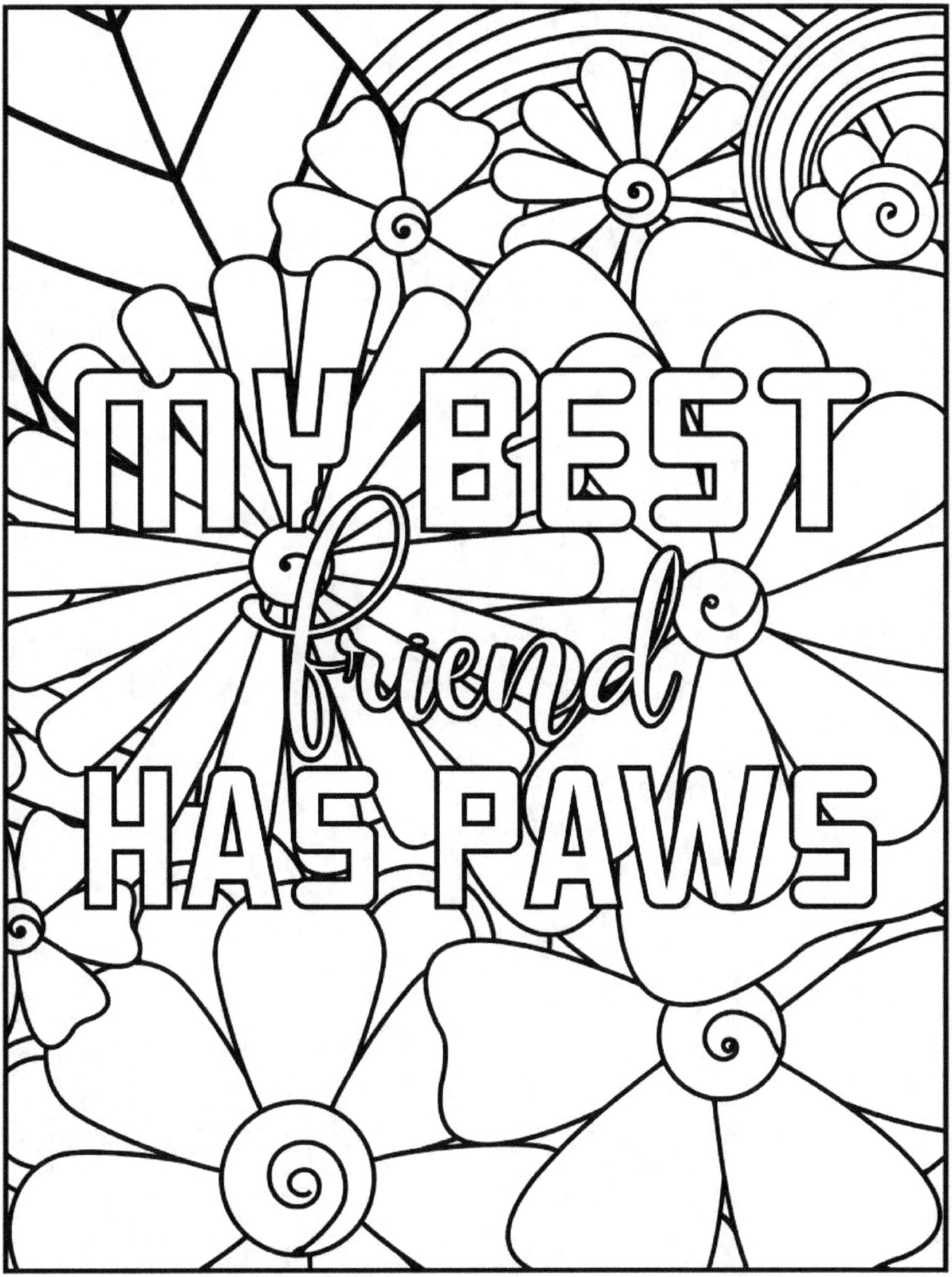
MY BEST
friend
HAS PAWS

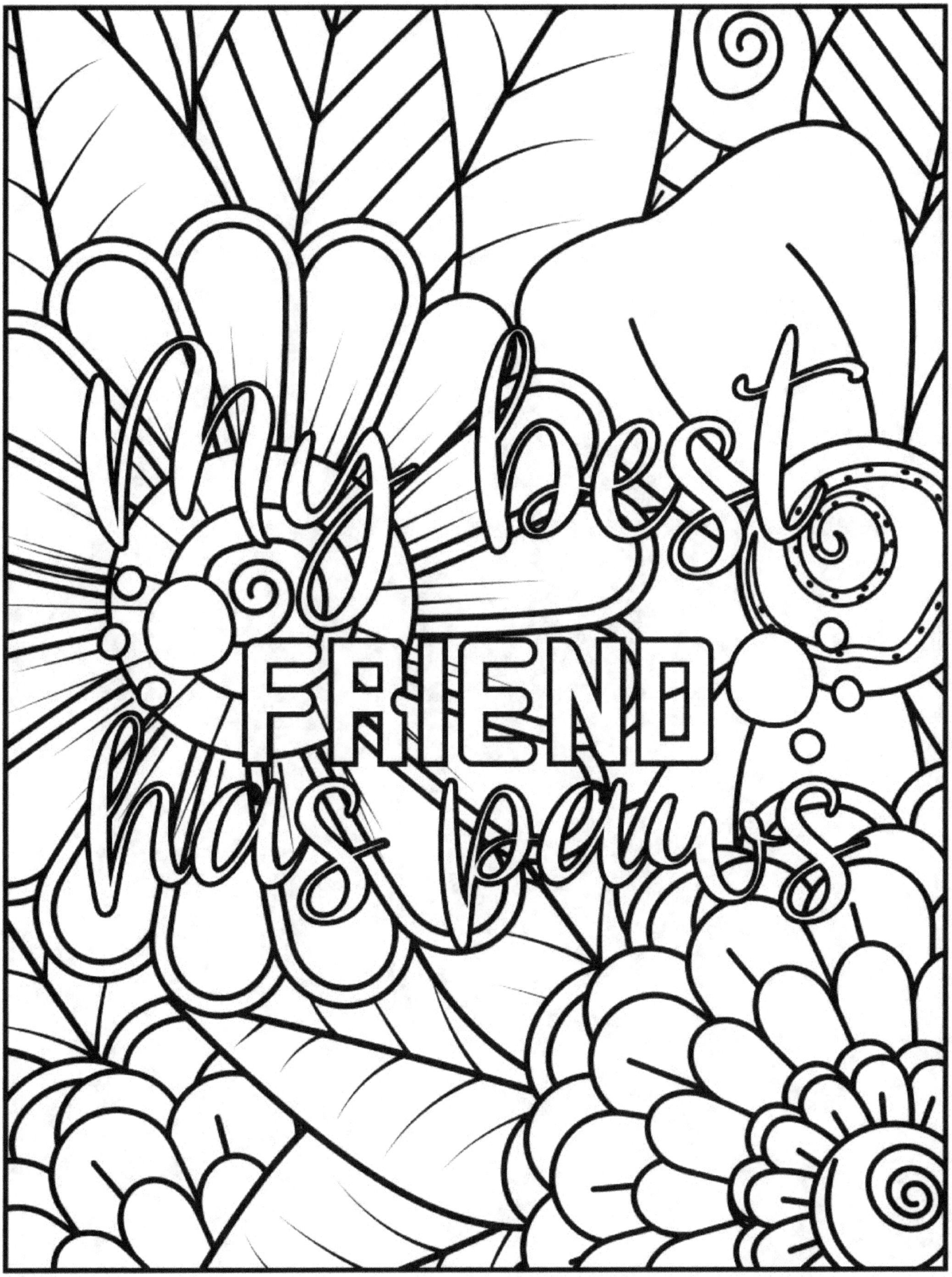
my best
FRIEND
has paws

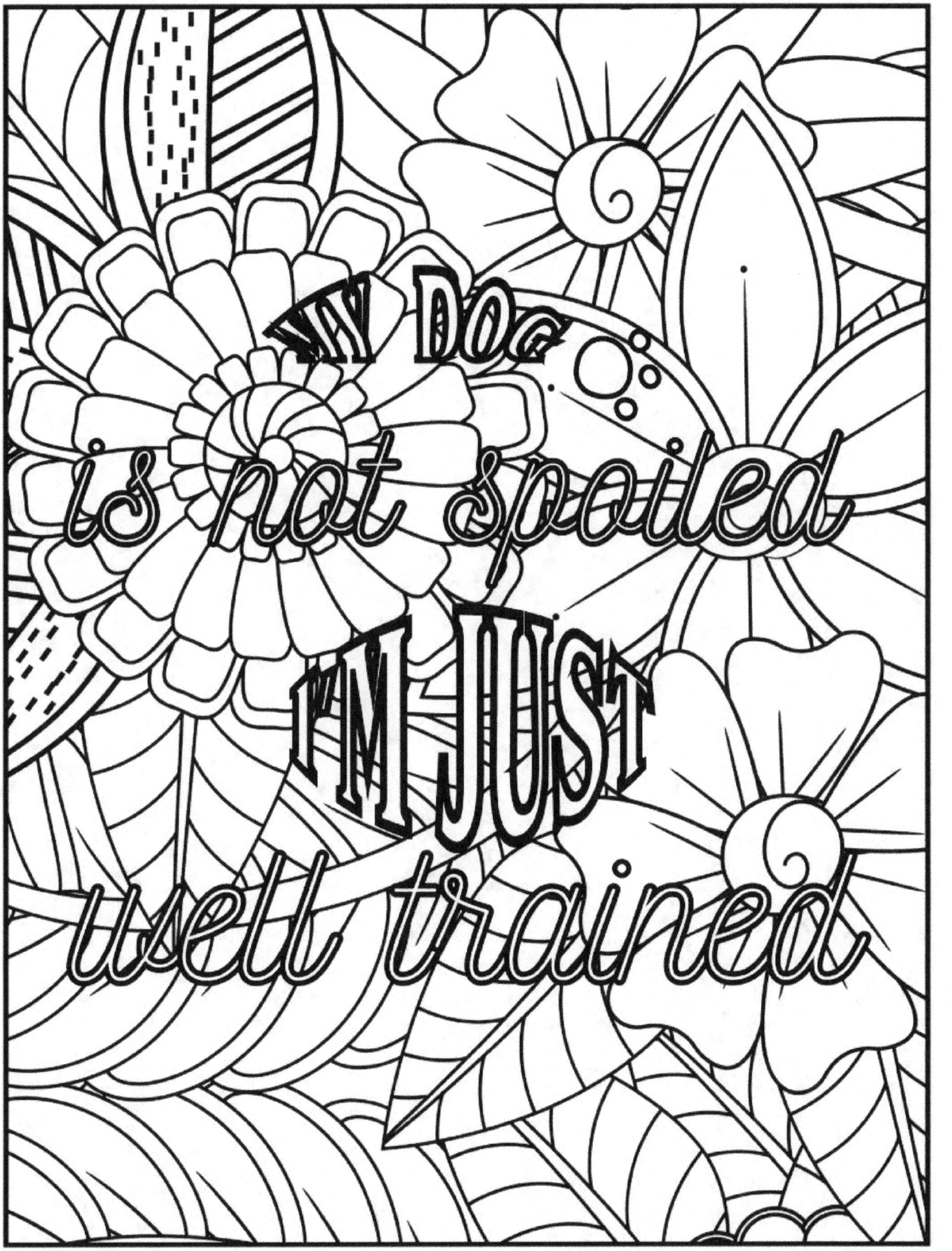
MY DOG
is not spoiled
I'M JUST
well trained

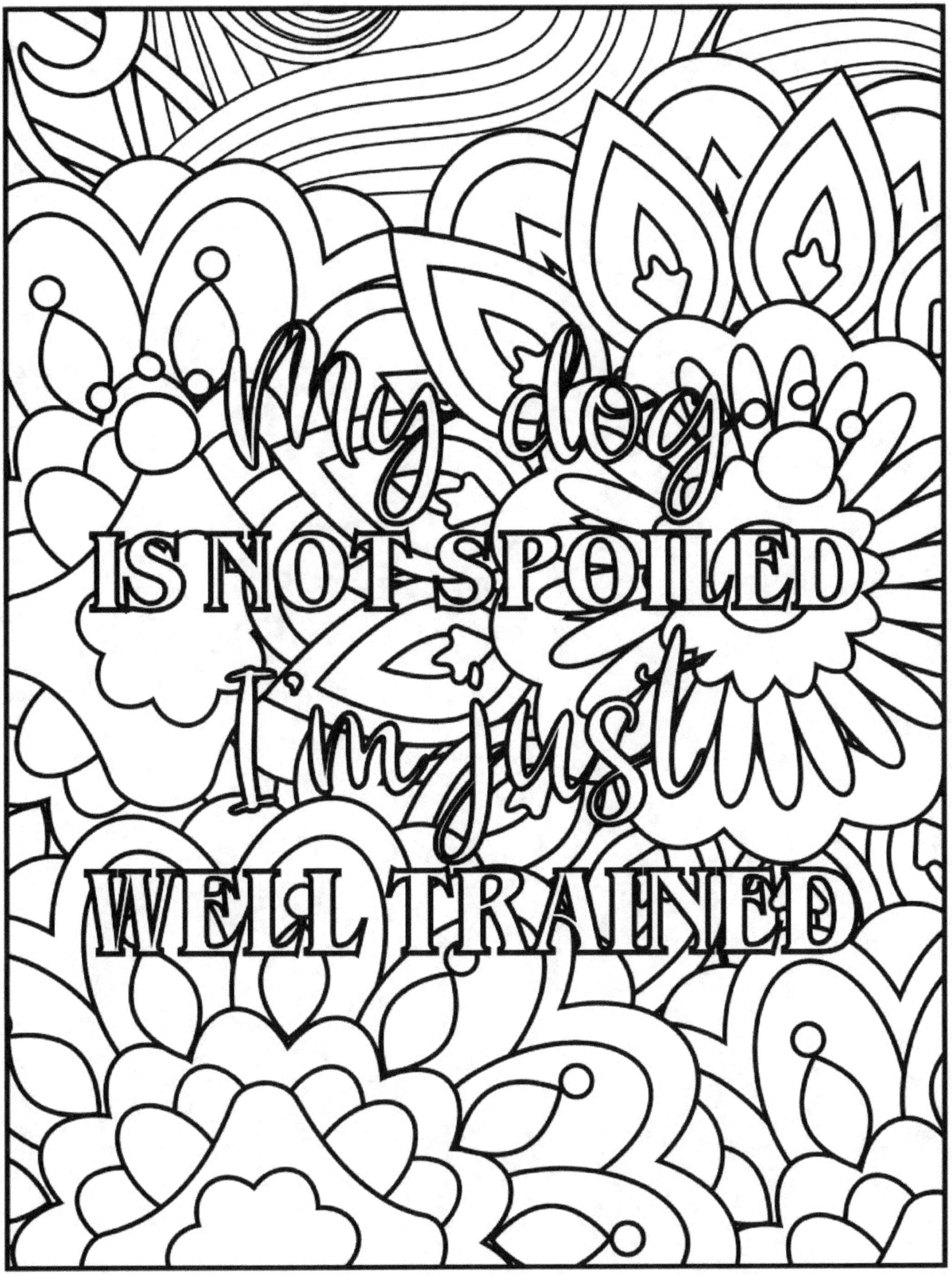
My dog
IS NOT SPOILED
I'm just
WELL TRAINED

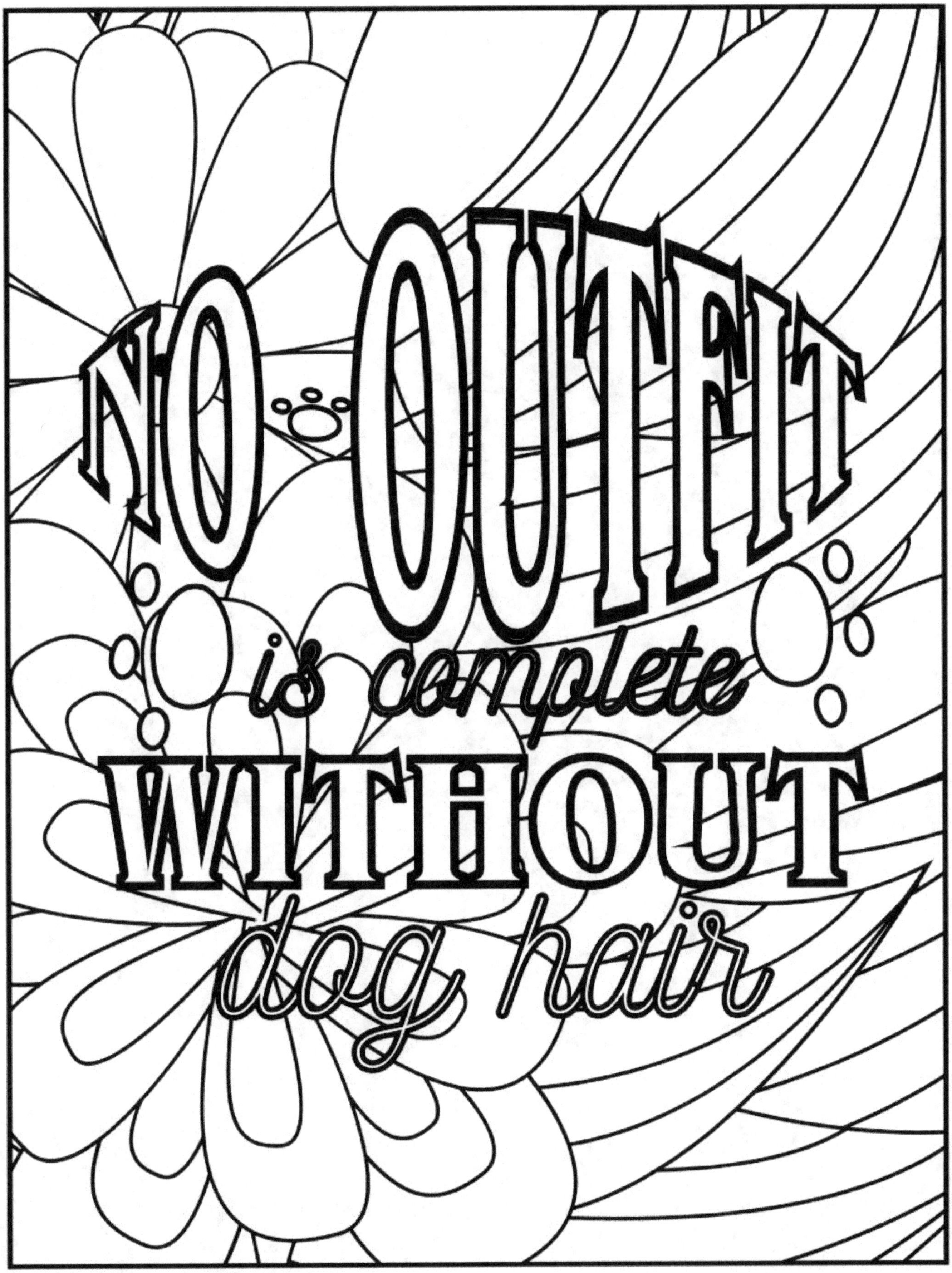
NO OUTFIT
is complete
WITHOUT
dog hair

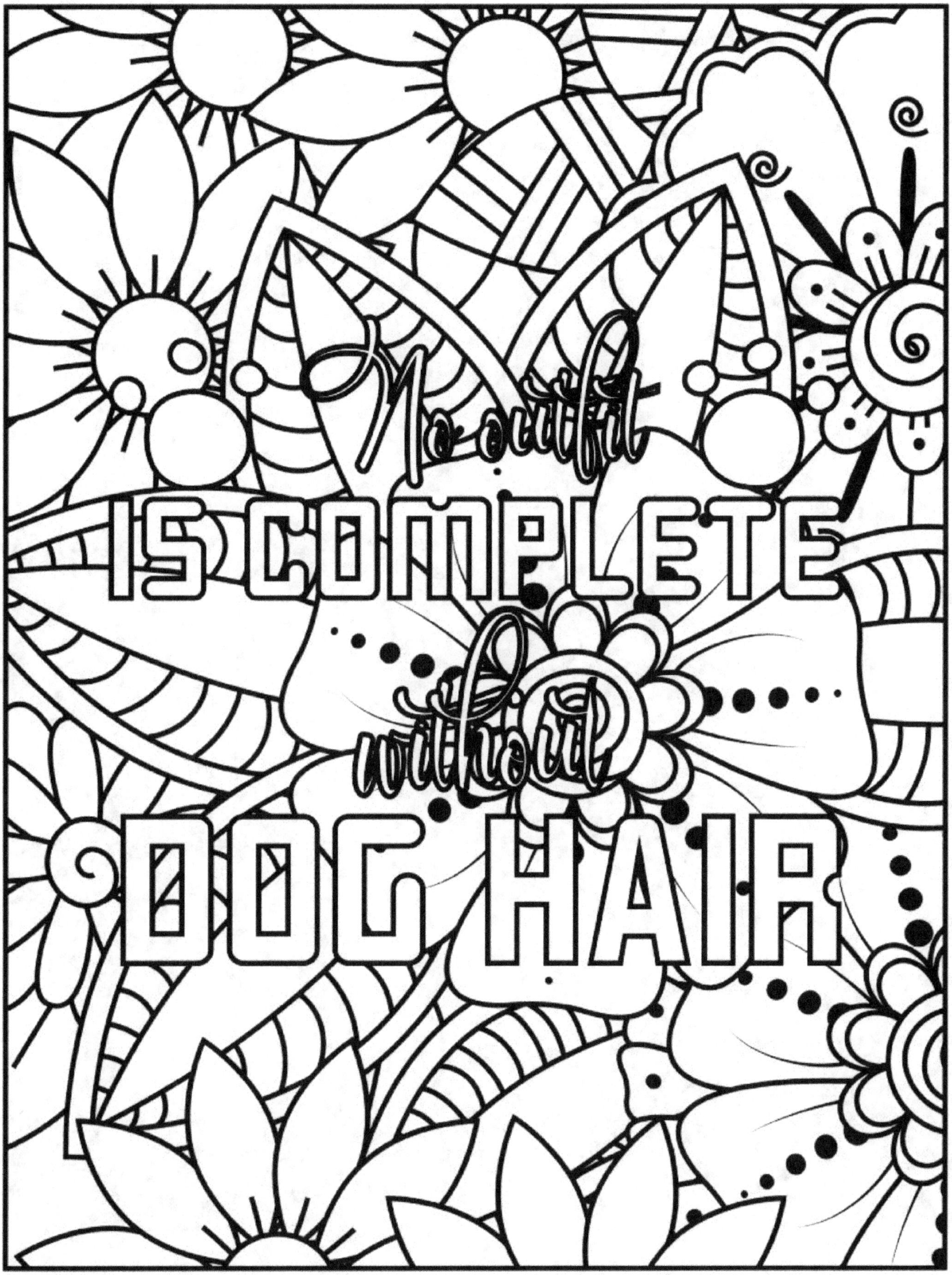
No outfit
IS COMPLETE
without
DOG HAIR

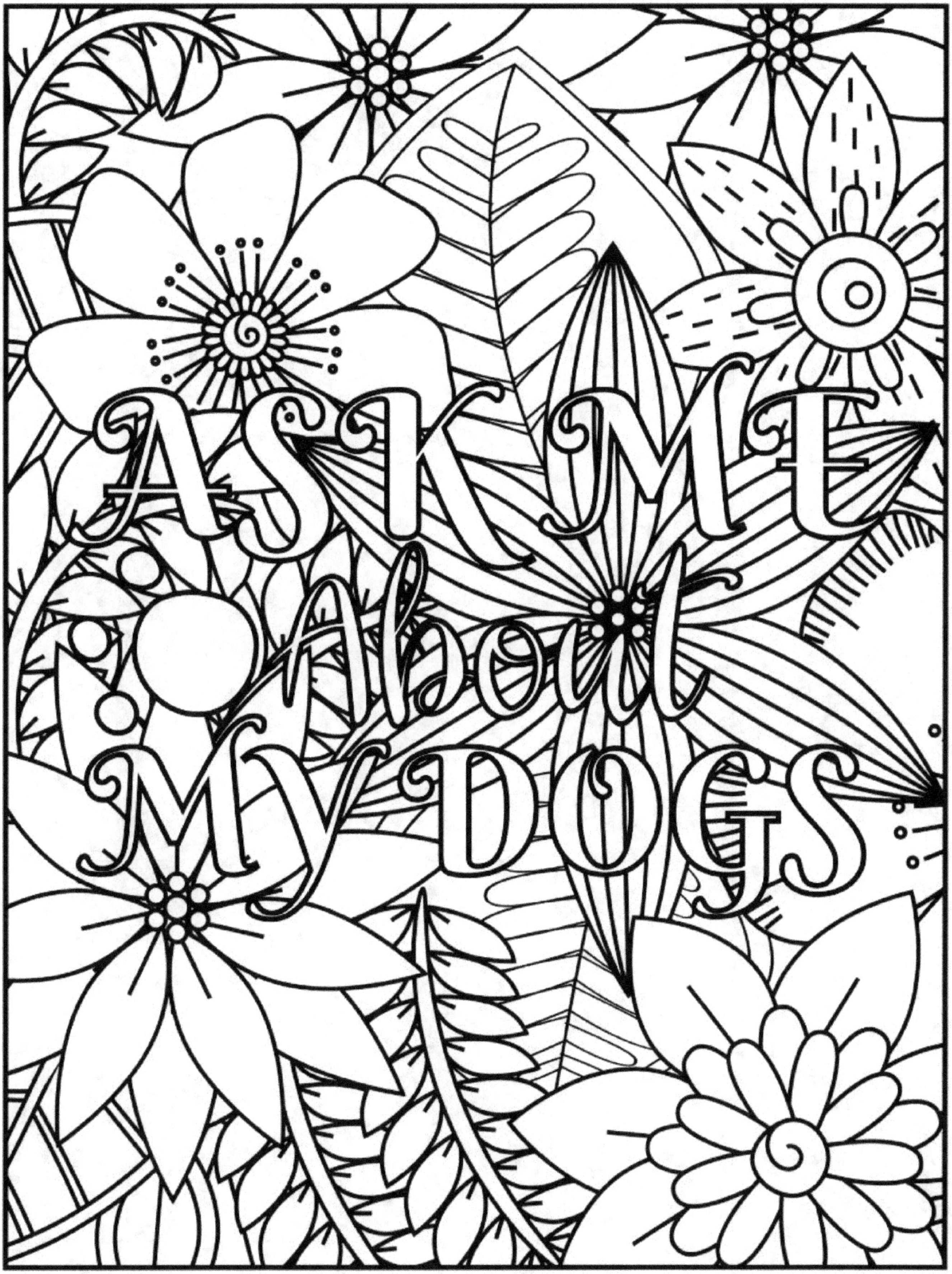
ASK ME
About
MY DOGS

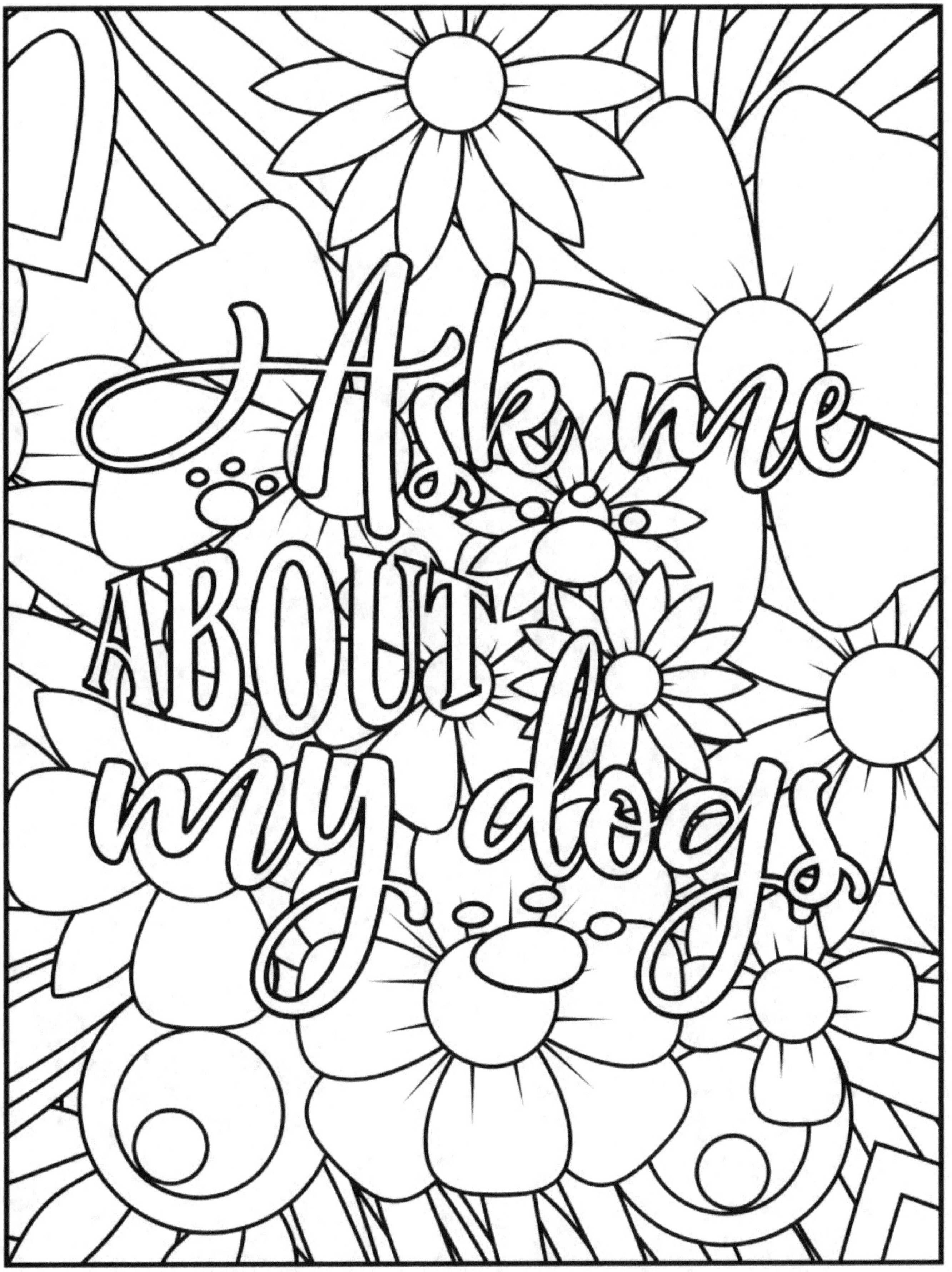
Ask me
ABOUT
my dogs

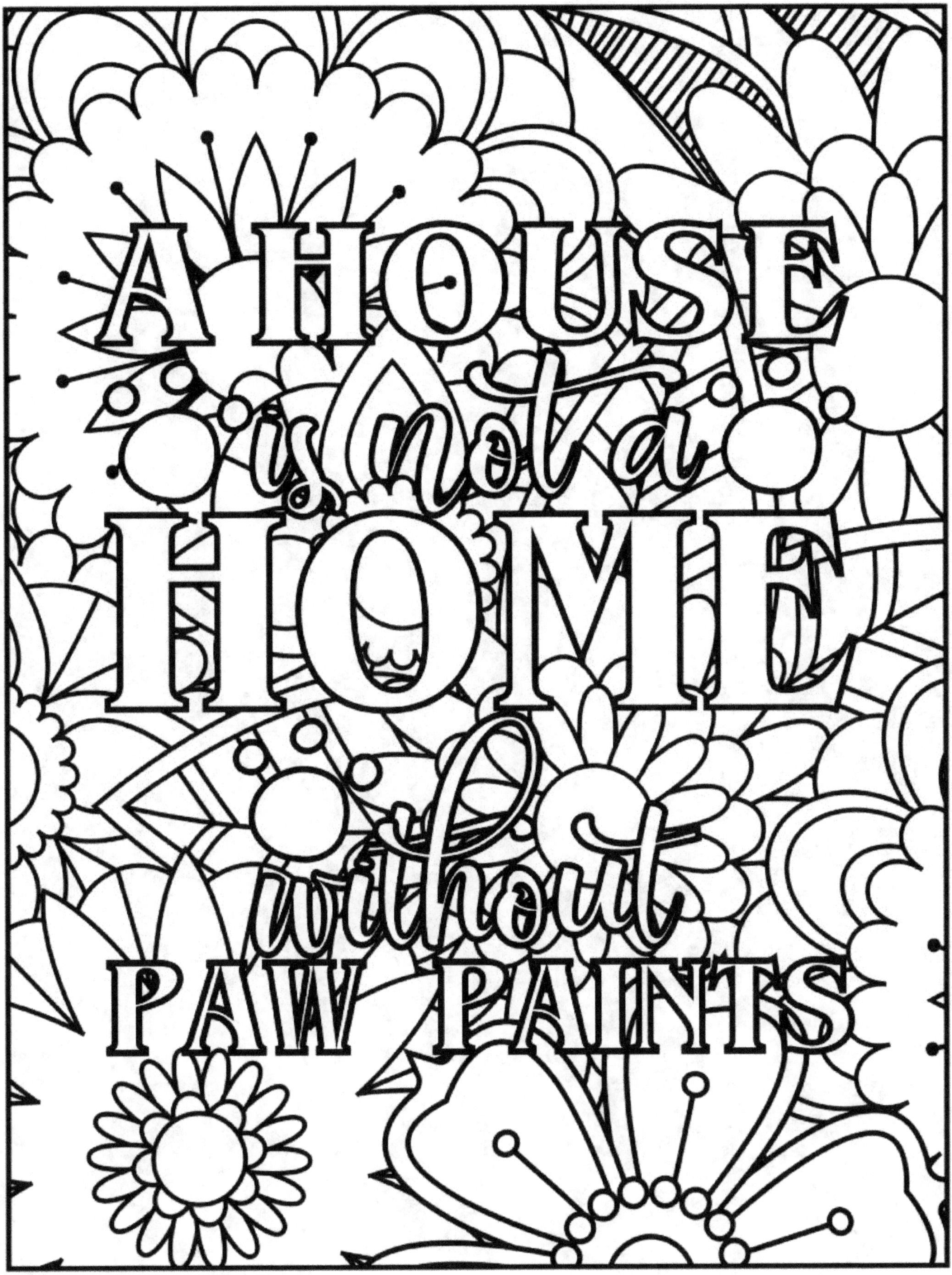
A HOUSE
is not a
HOME
without
PAW PAINTS

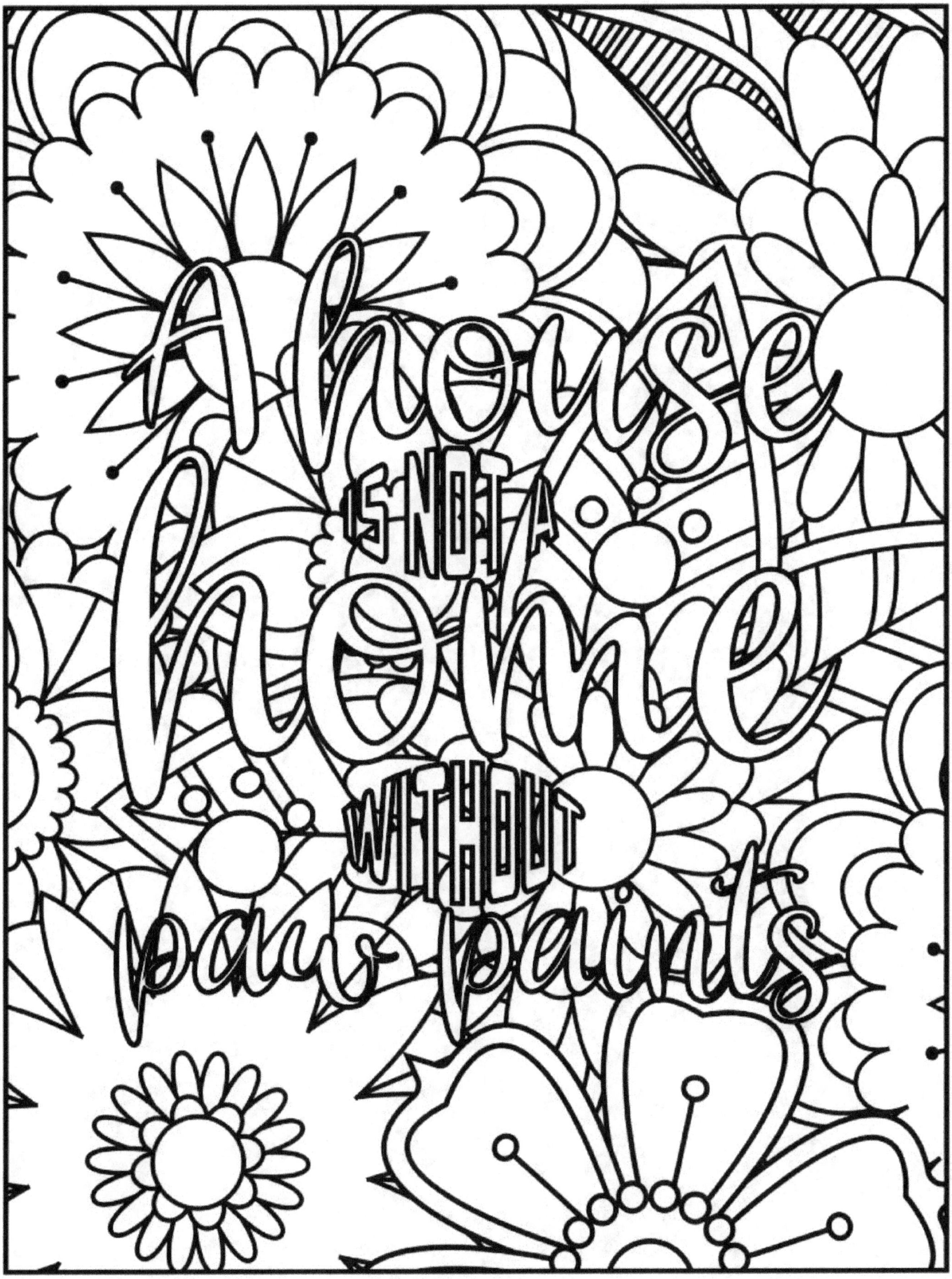
A house
IS NOT A
home
WITHOUT
paw paints

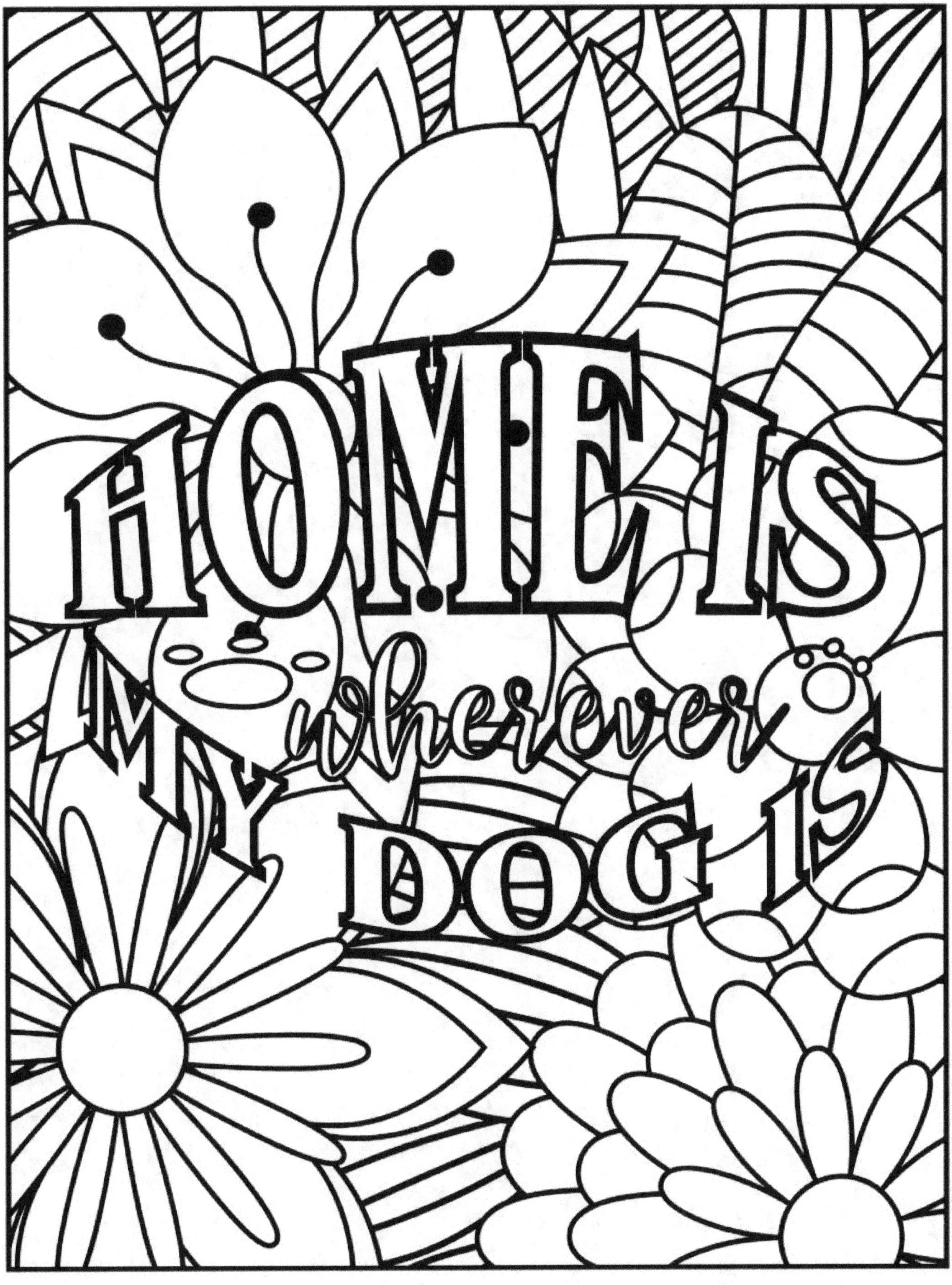
HOME IS
wherever
MY DOG IS

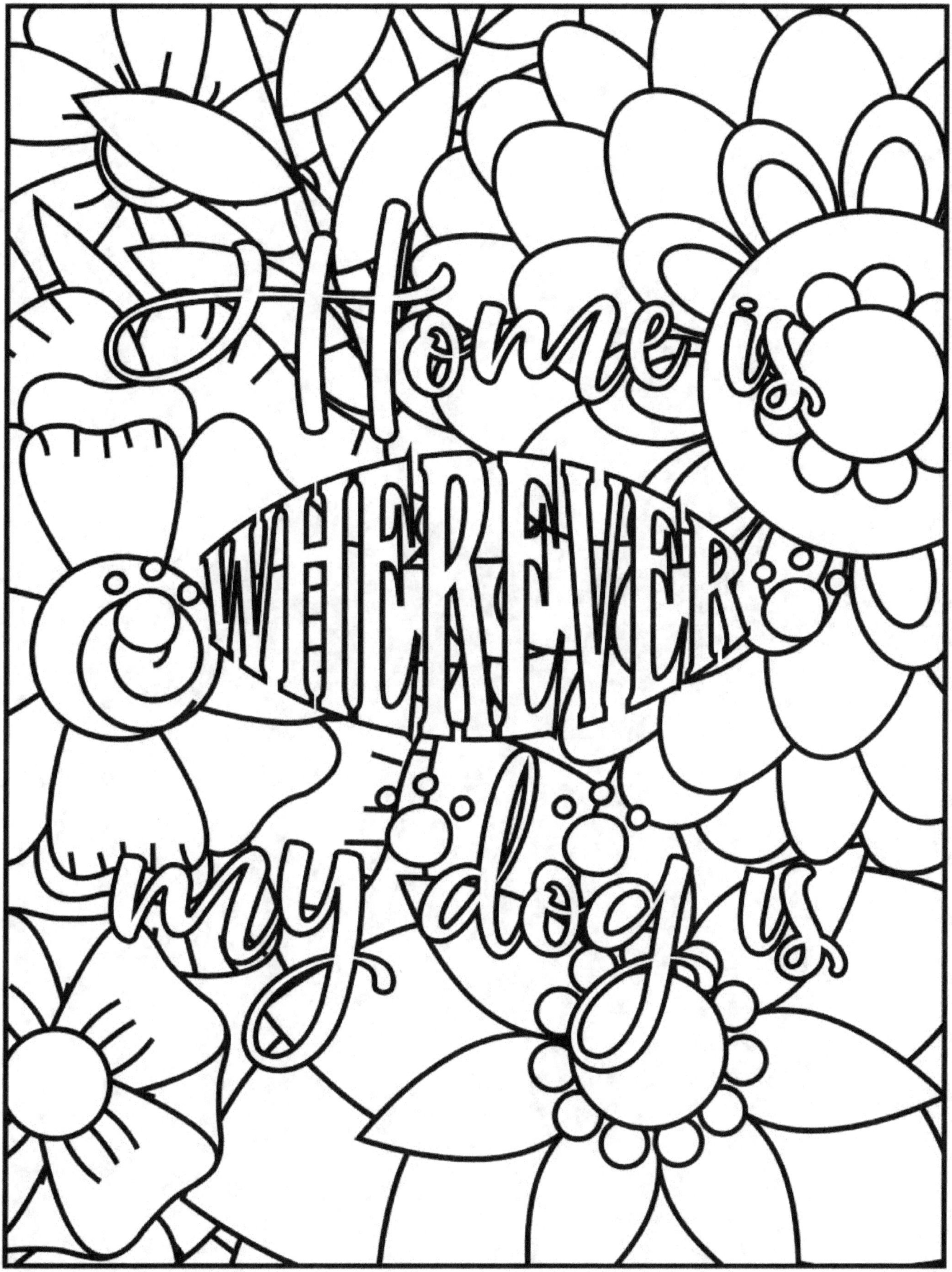
Home is
WHEREVER
my dog is

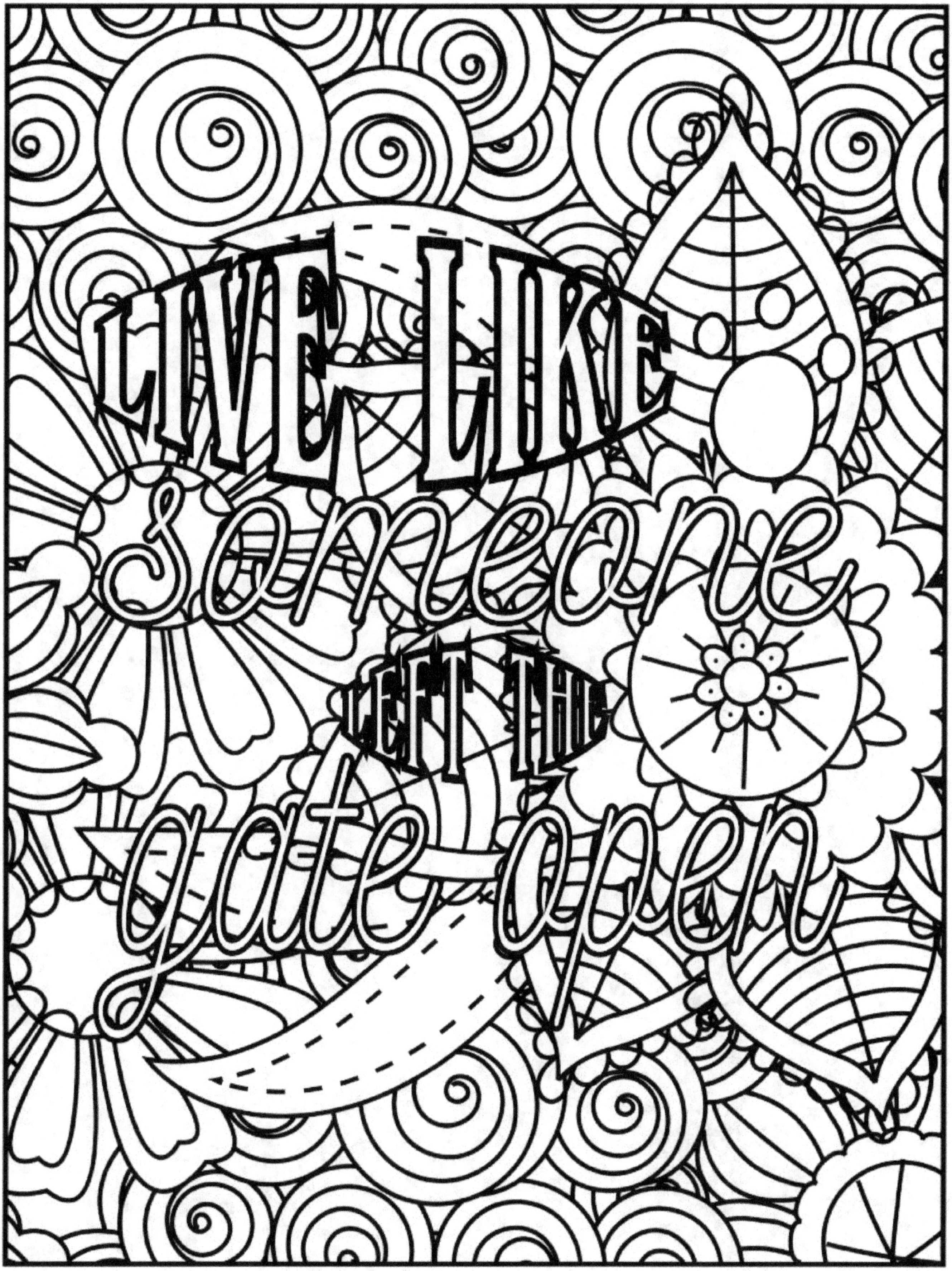
LIVE LIKE
someone
LEFT THE
gate open

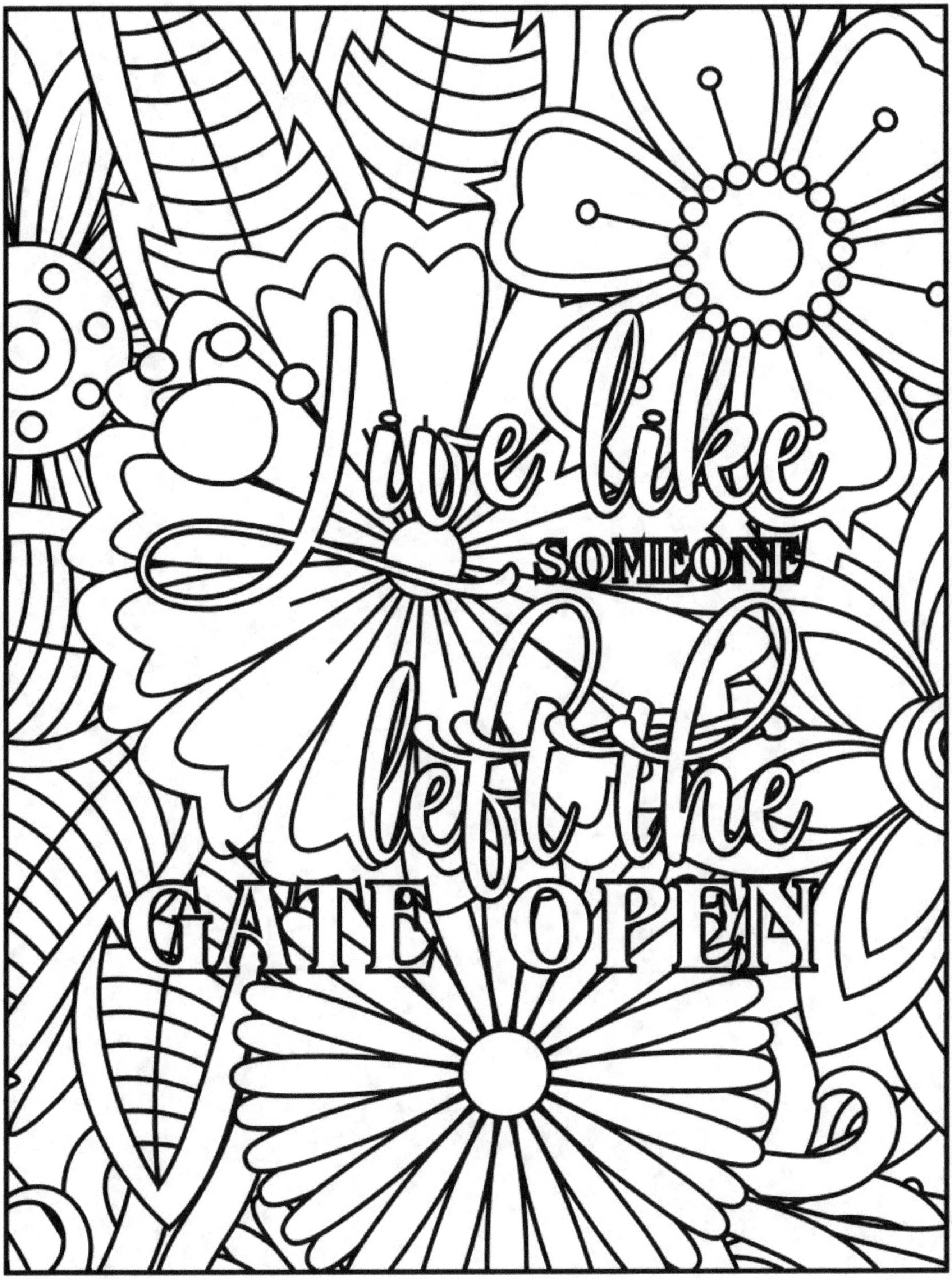
Live like
SOMEONE
left the
GATE OPEN

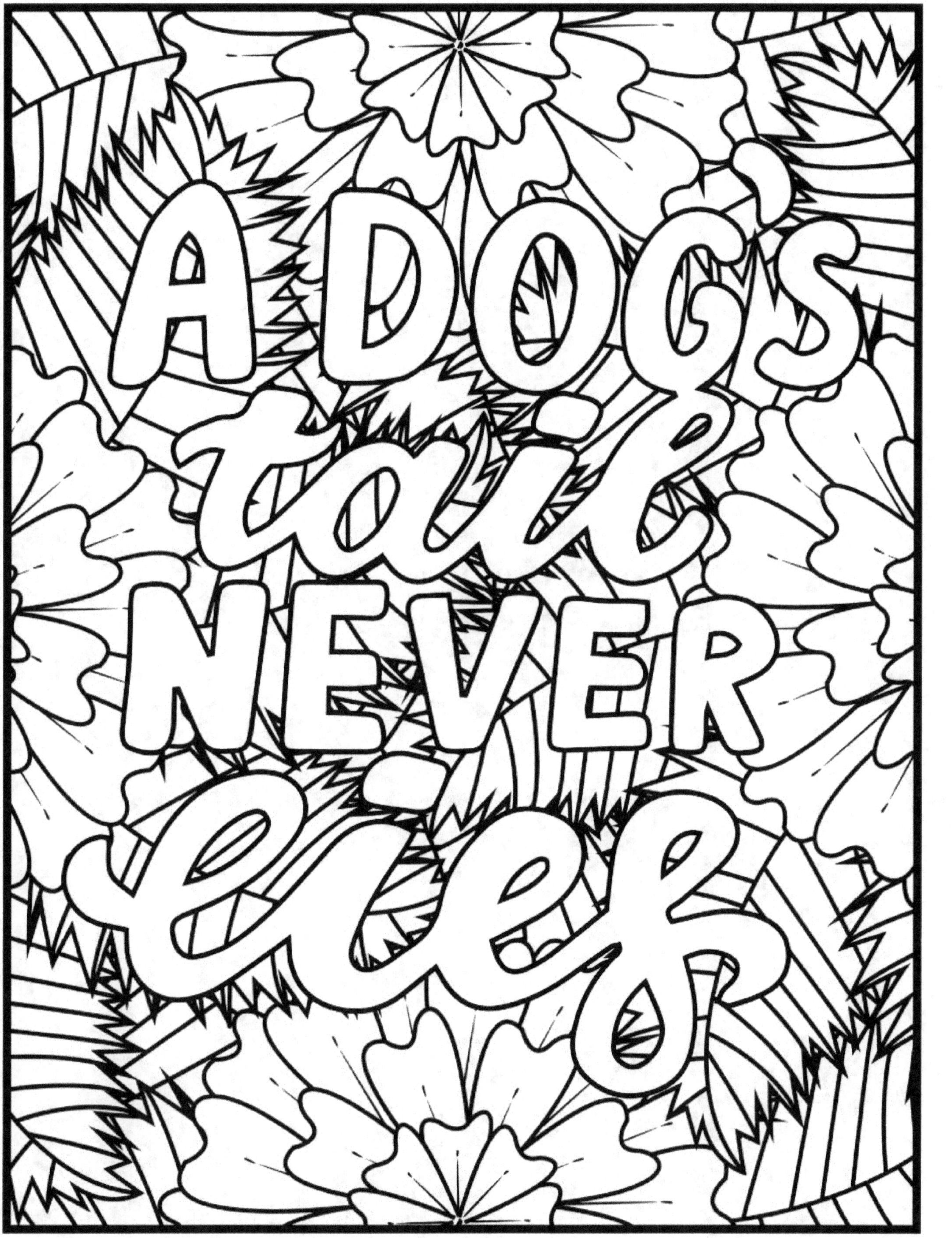
A DOG'S
tail
NEVER
lies

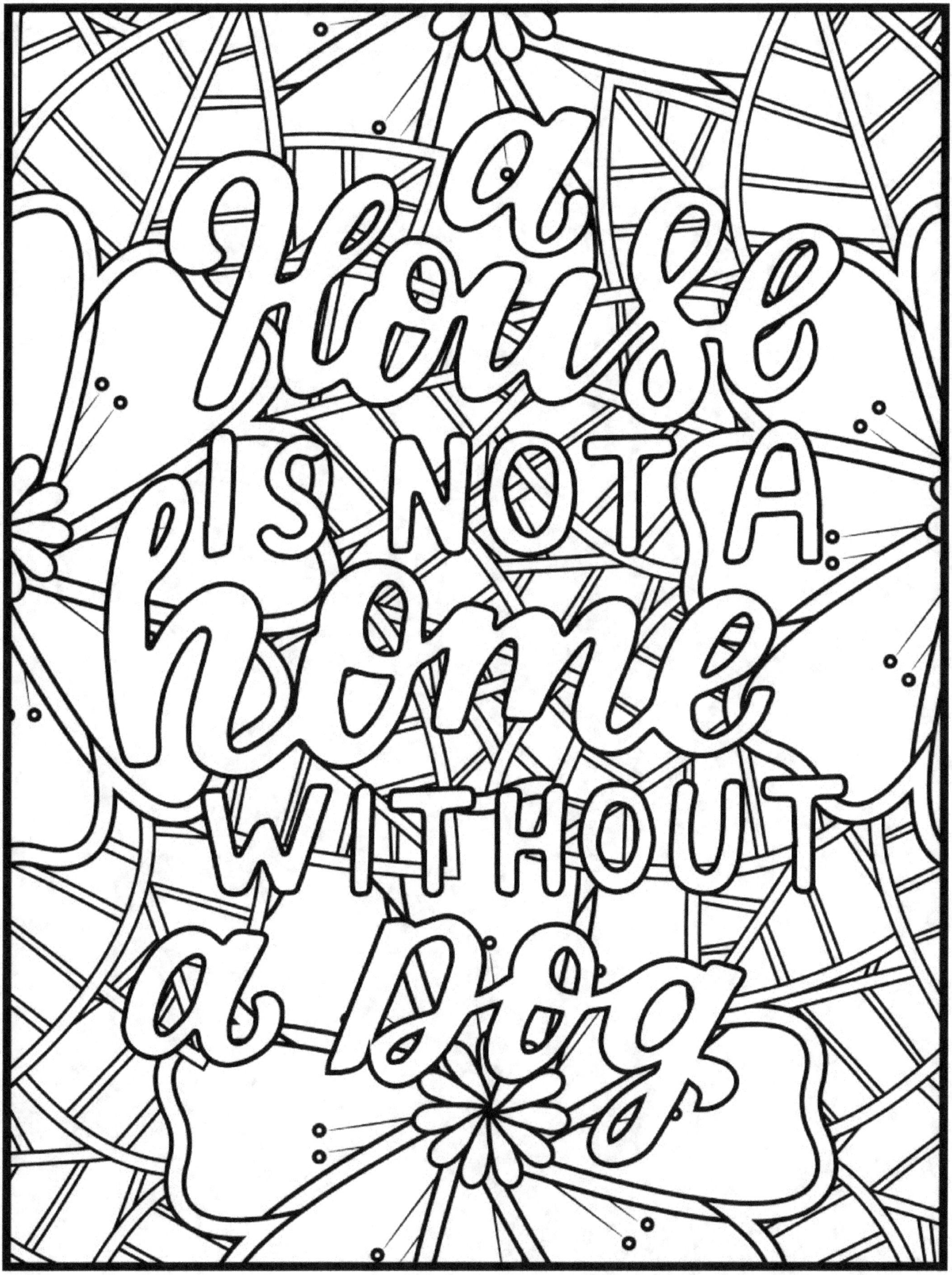
a House
IS NOT A
home
WITHOUT
a Dog

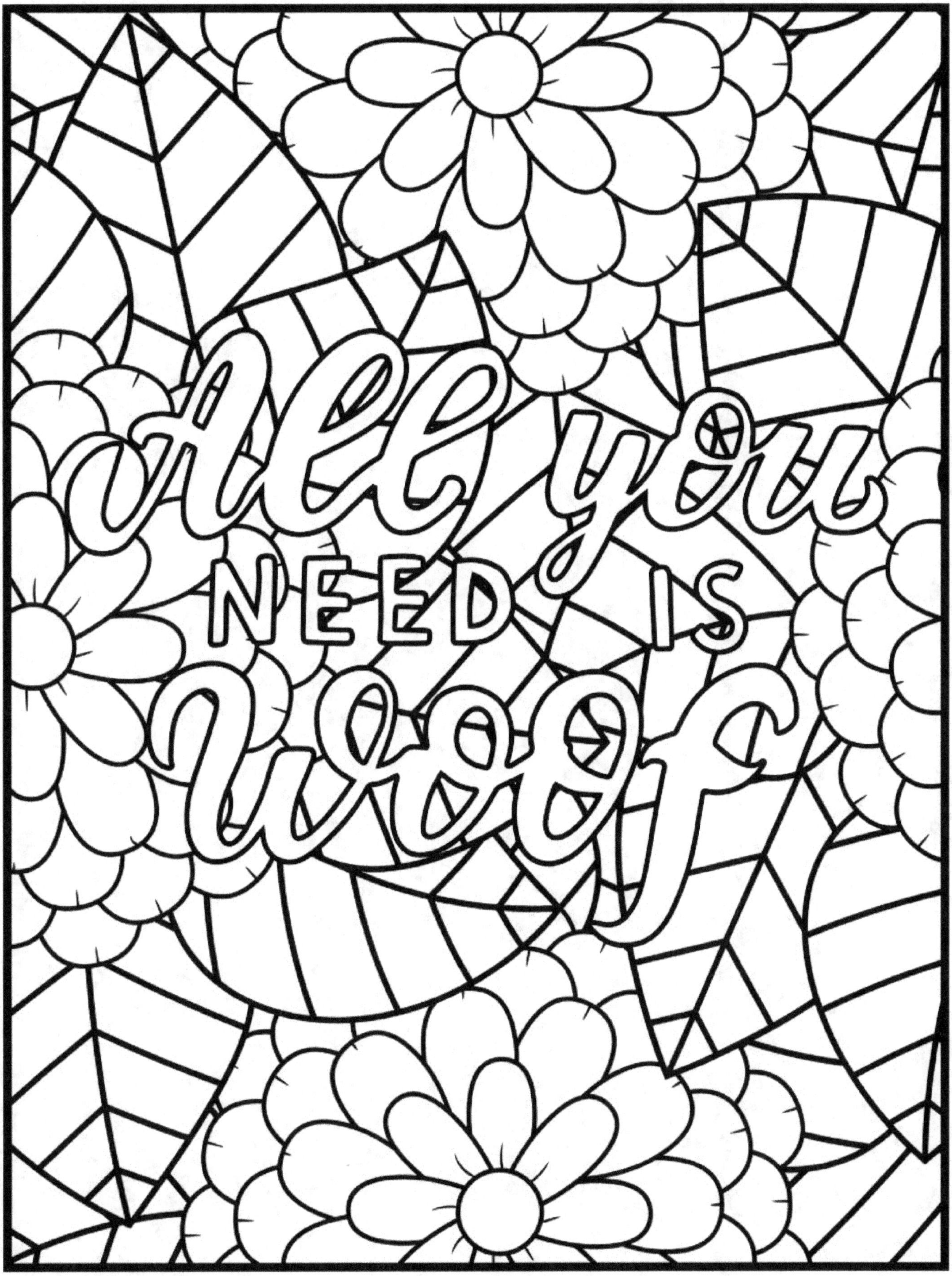
All you
NEED IS
woof

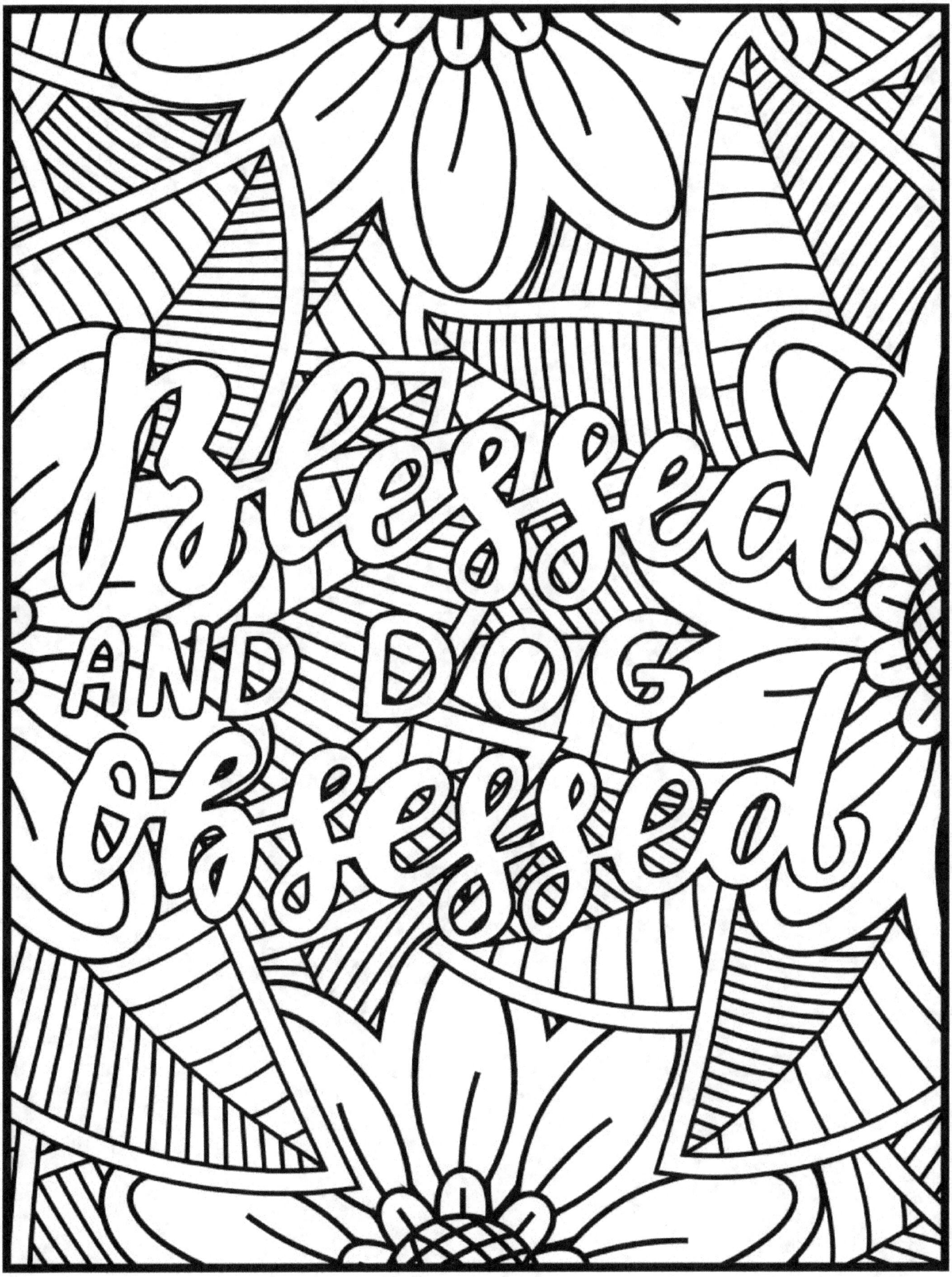
Blessed
AND DOG
obsessed

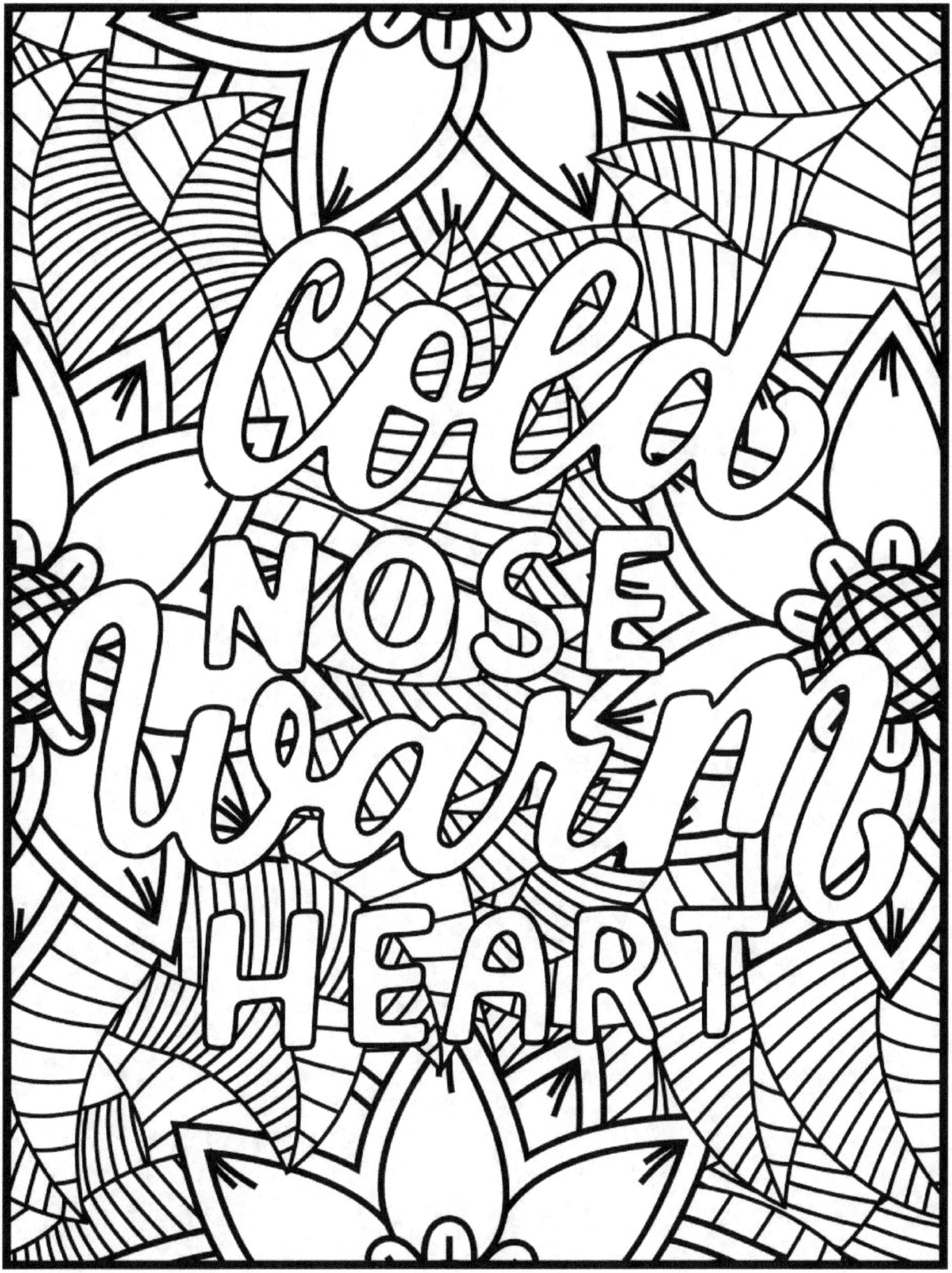
Cold
NOSE
warm
HEART

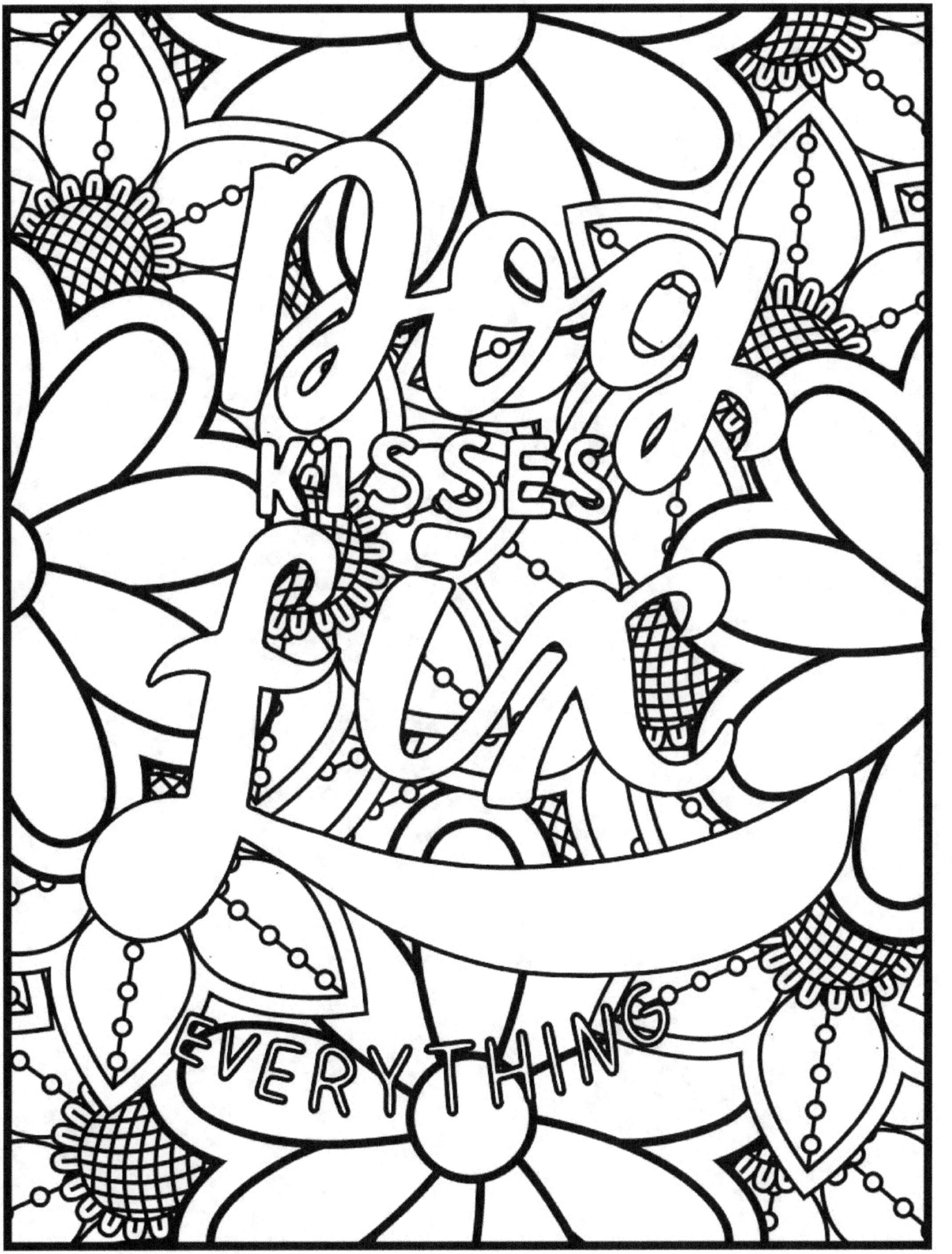
Dog
KISSES
fix
EVERYTHING

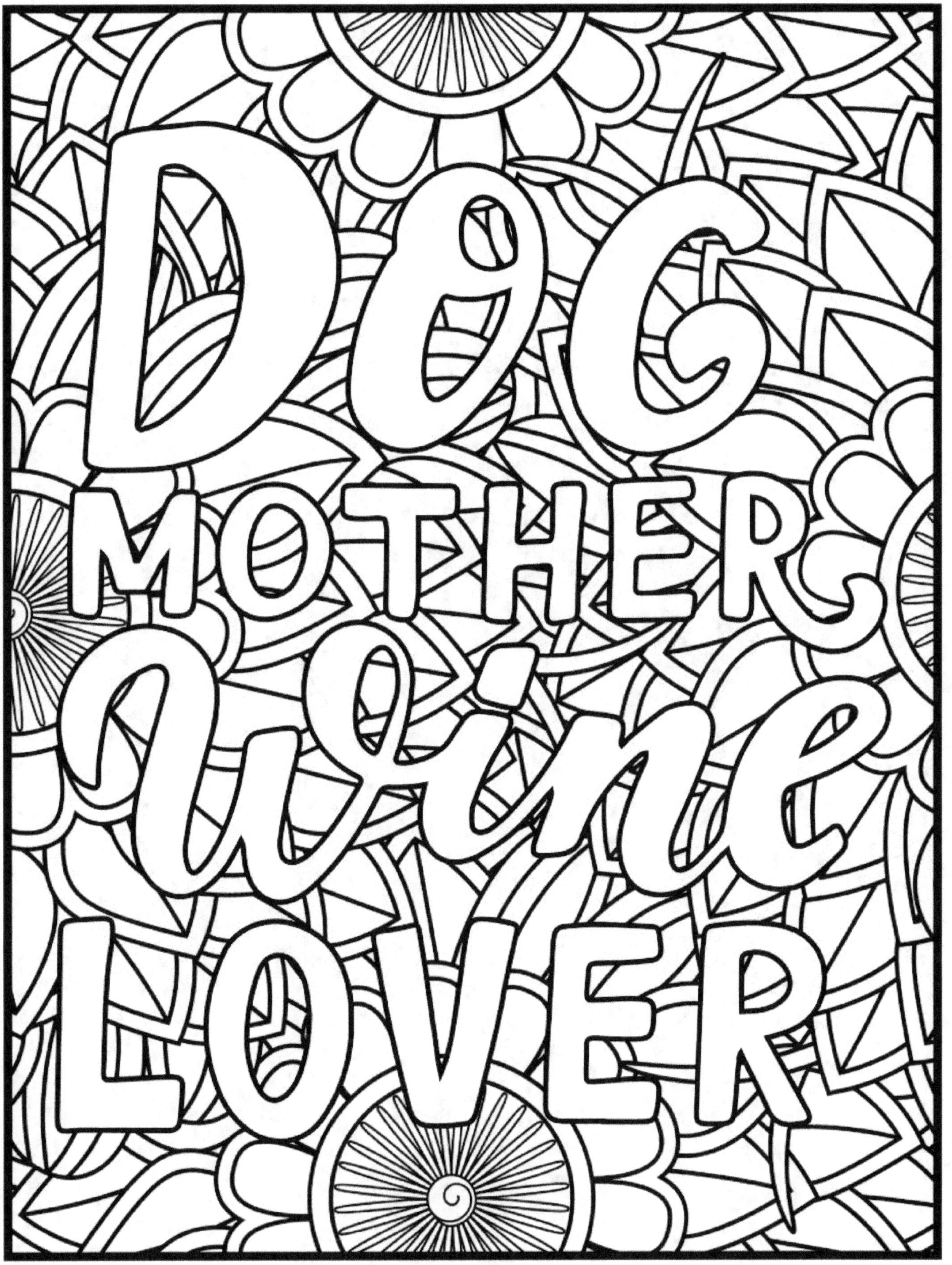
Dog
MOTHER
wine
LOVER

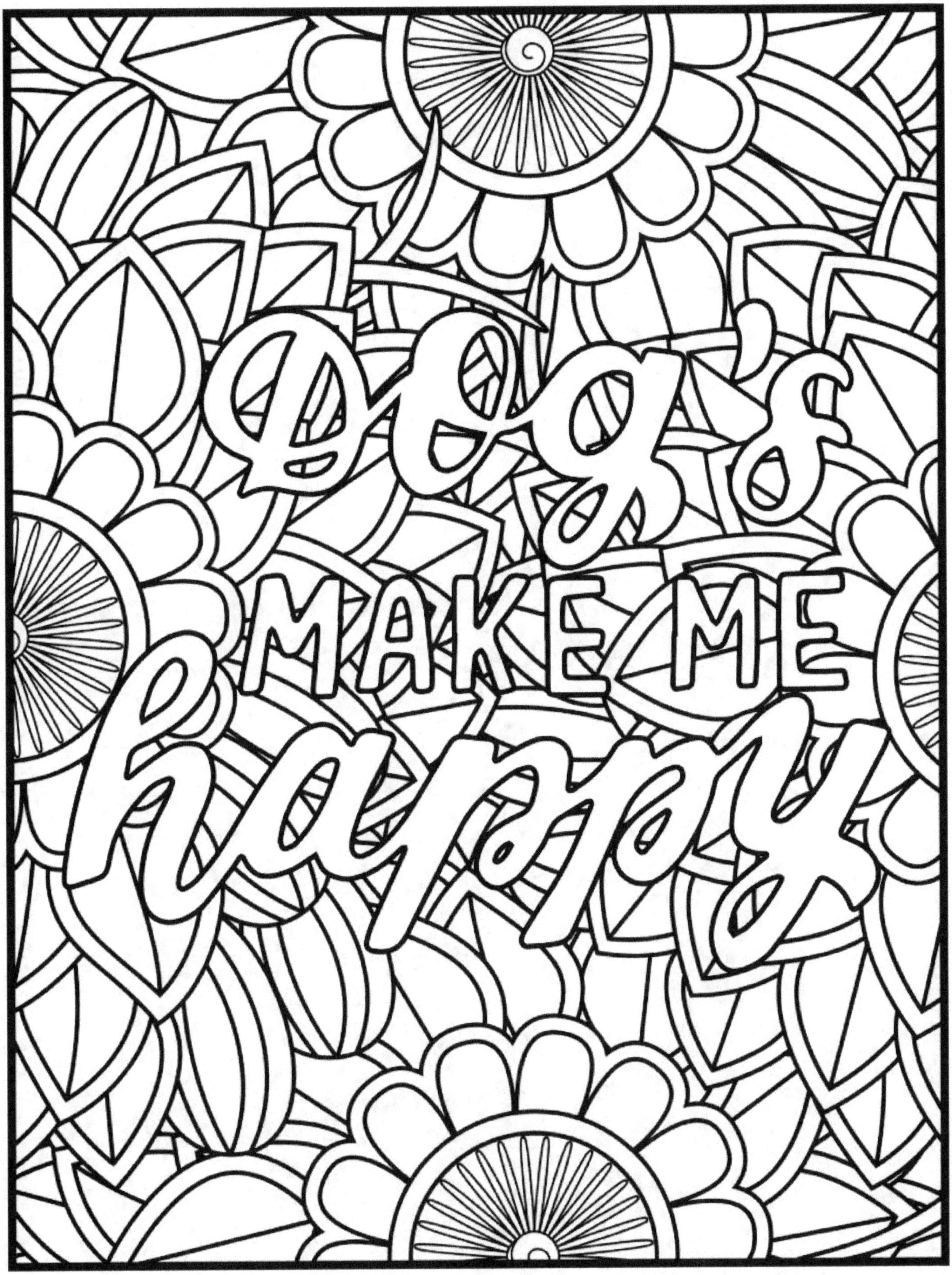
Dog's
MAKE ME
happy

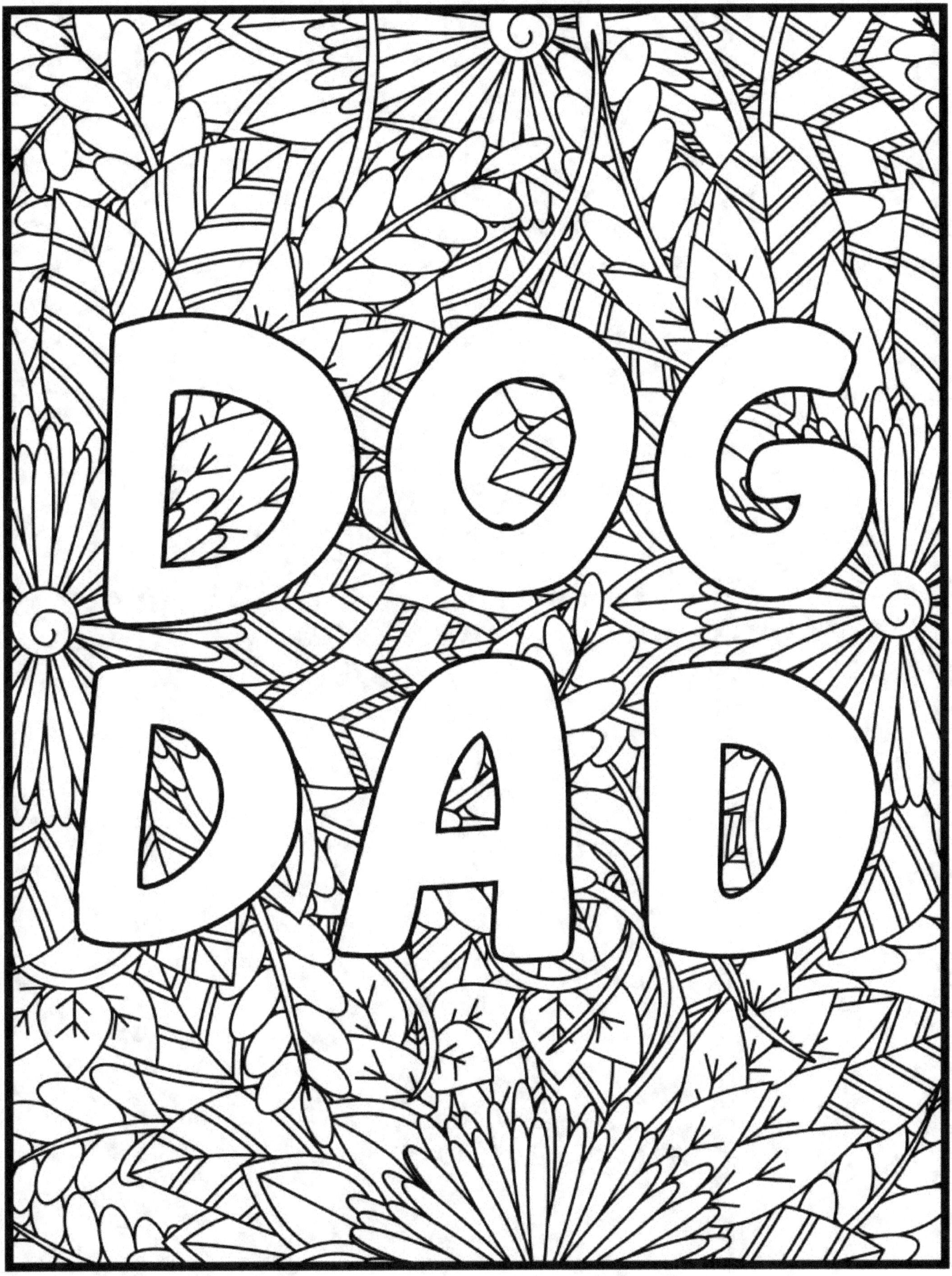
DOG
DAD

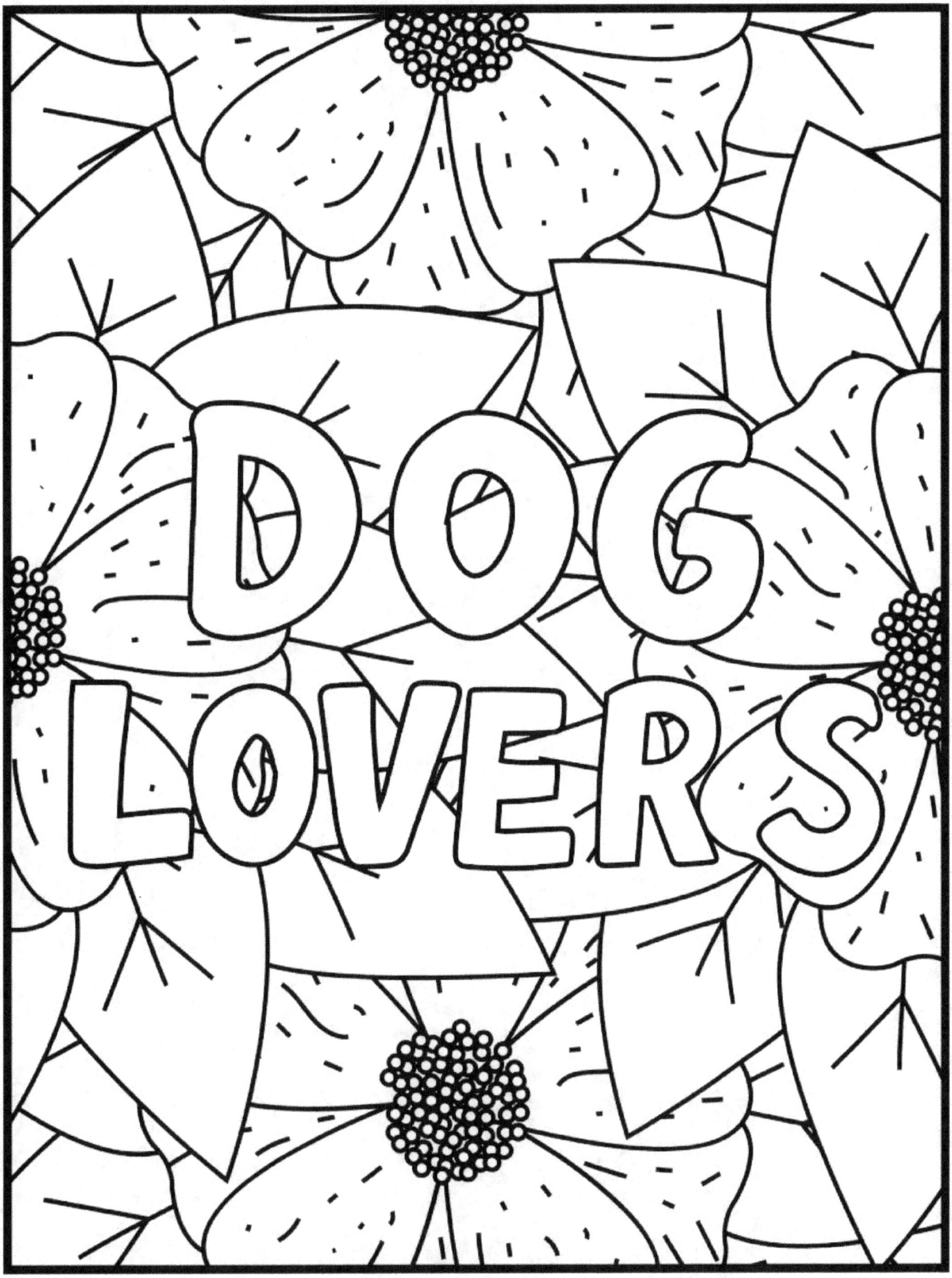
DOG
LOVERS

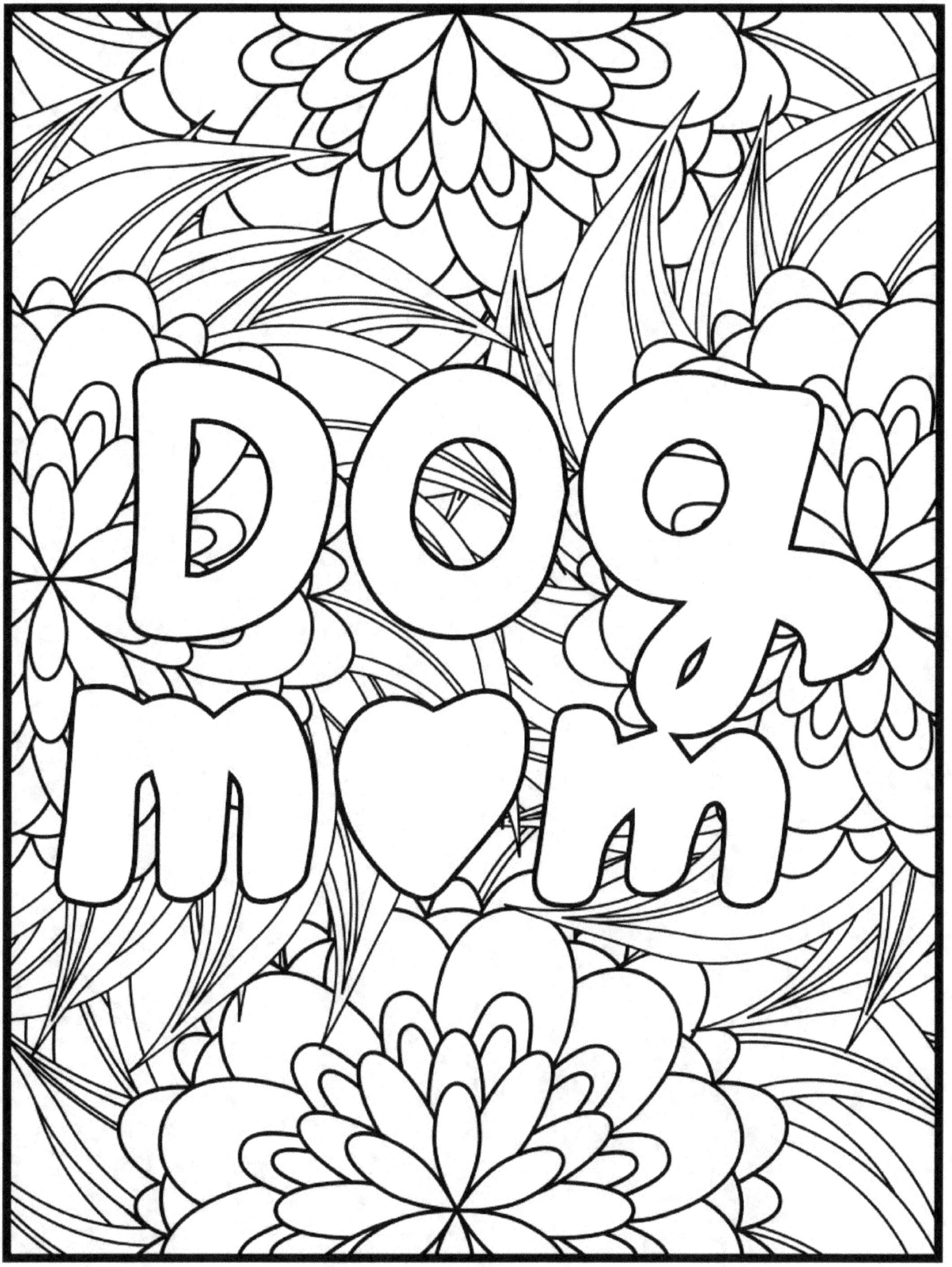
Dog
m♥m

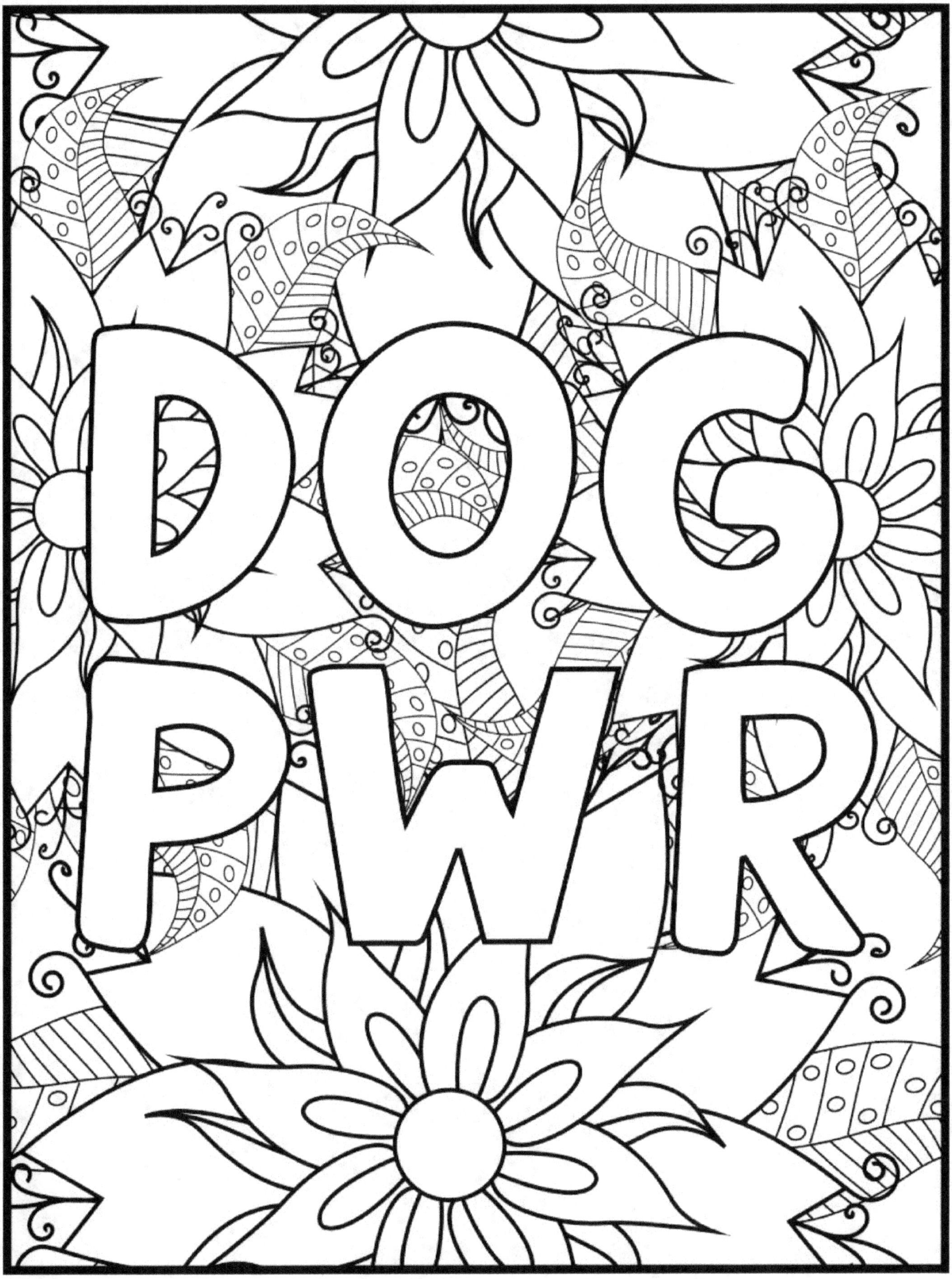
DOG
PWR

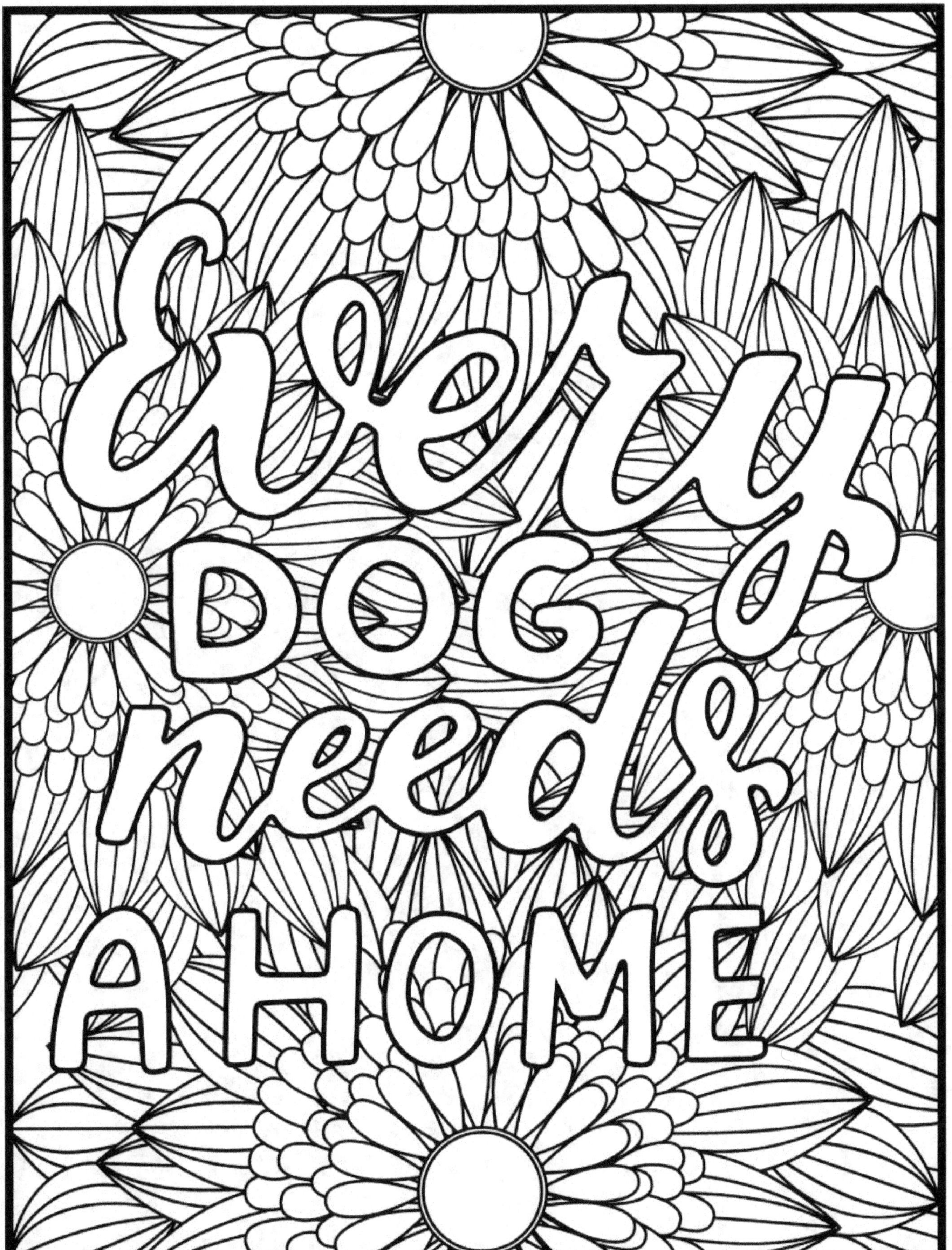
Every
DOG
needs
A HOME

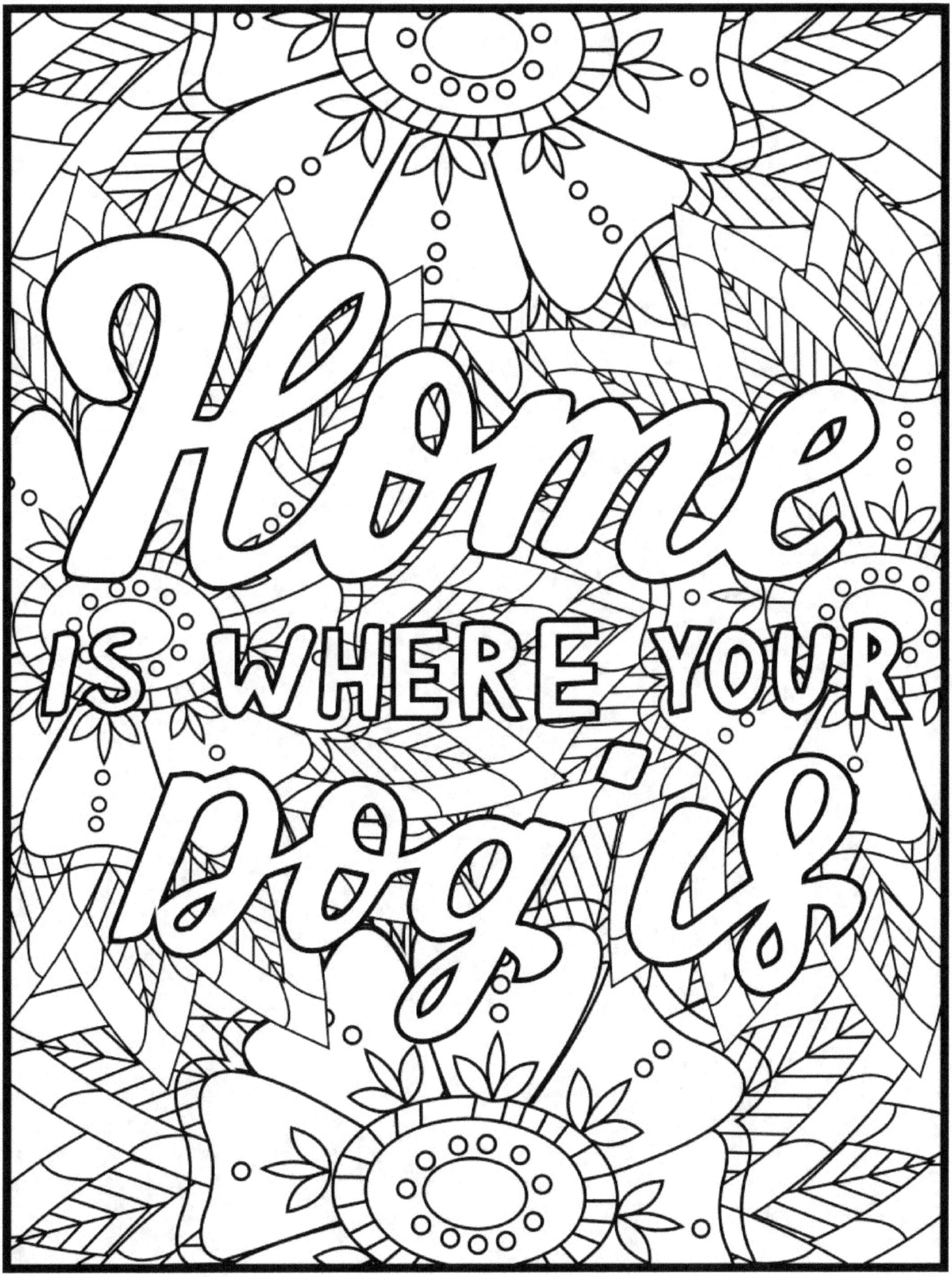
Home
is where your
Dog is

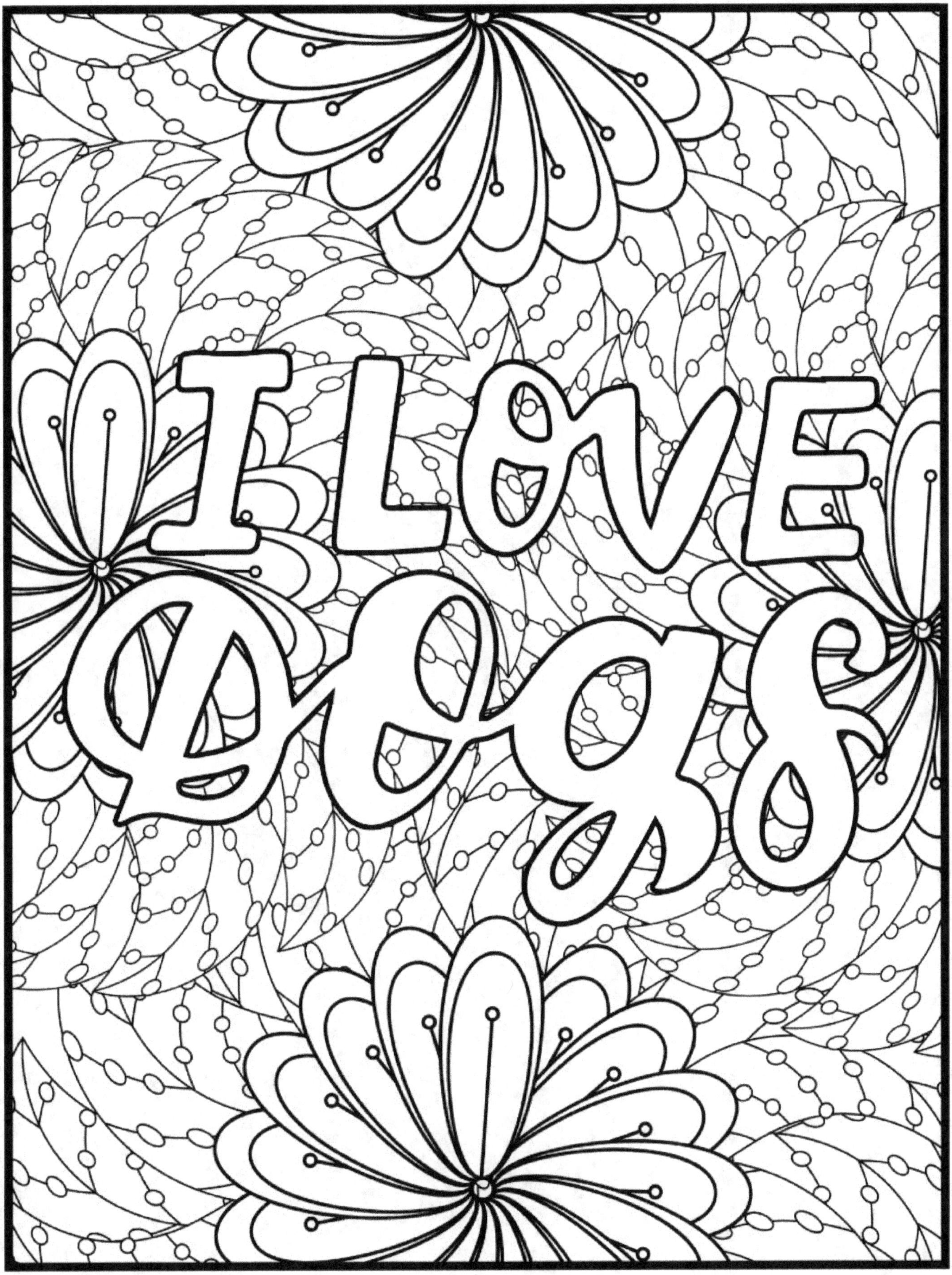
I Love
Dogs

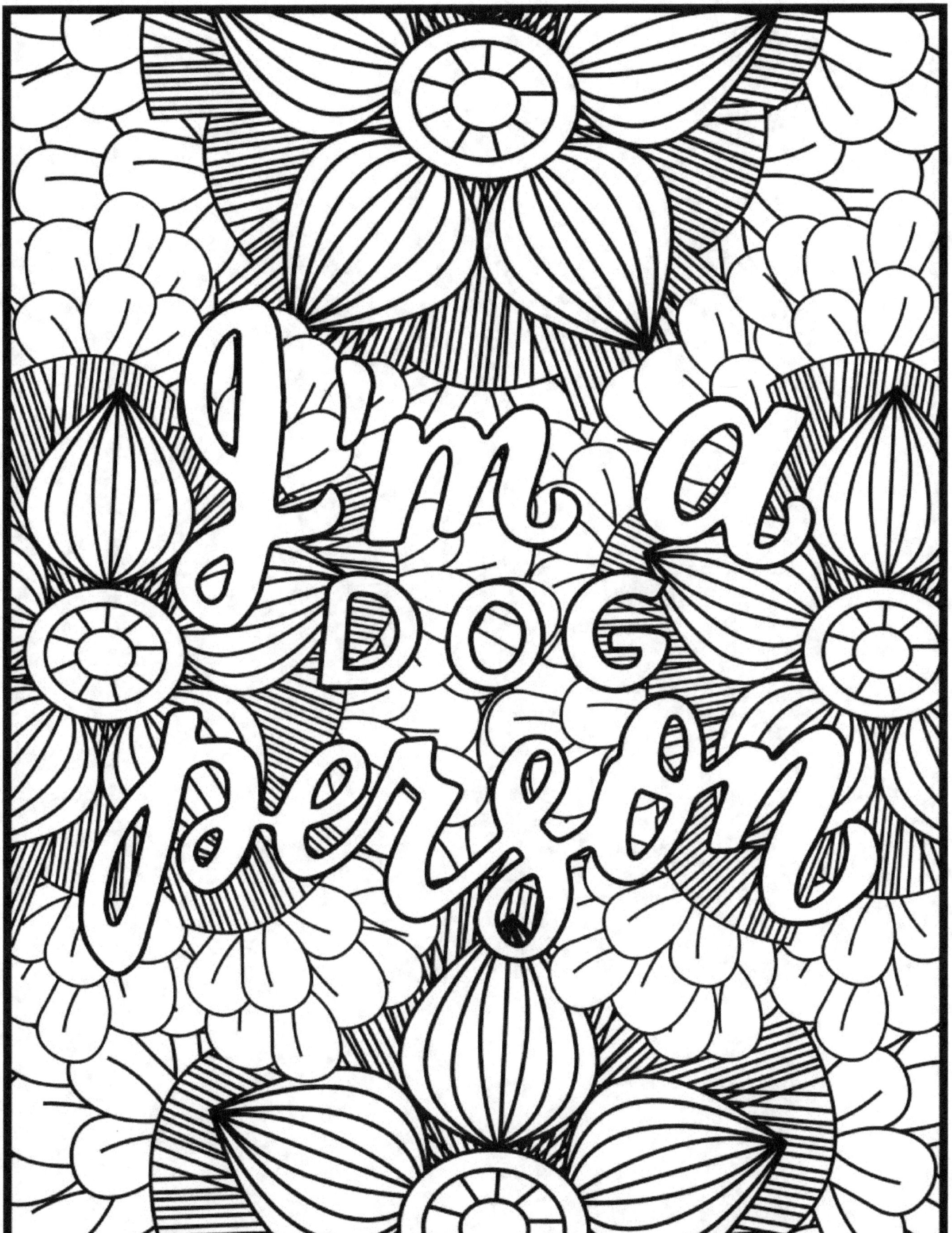
I'm a
DOG
person

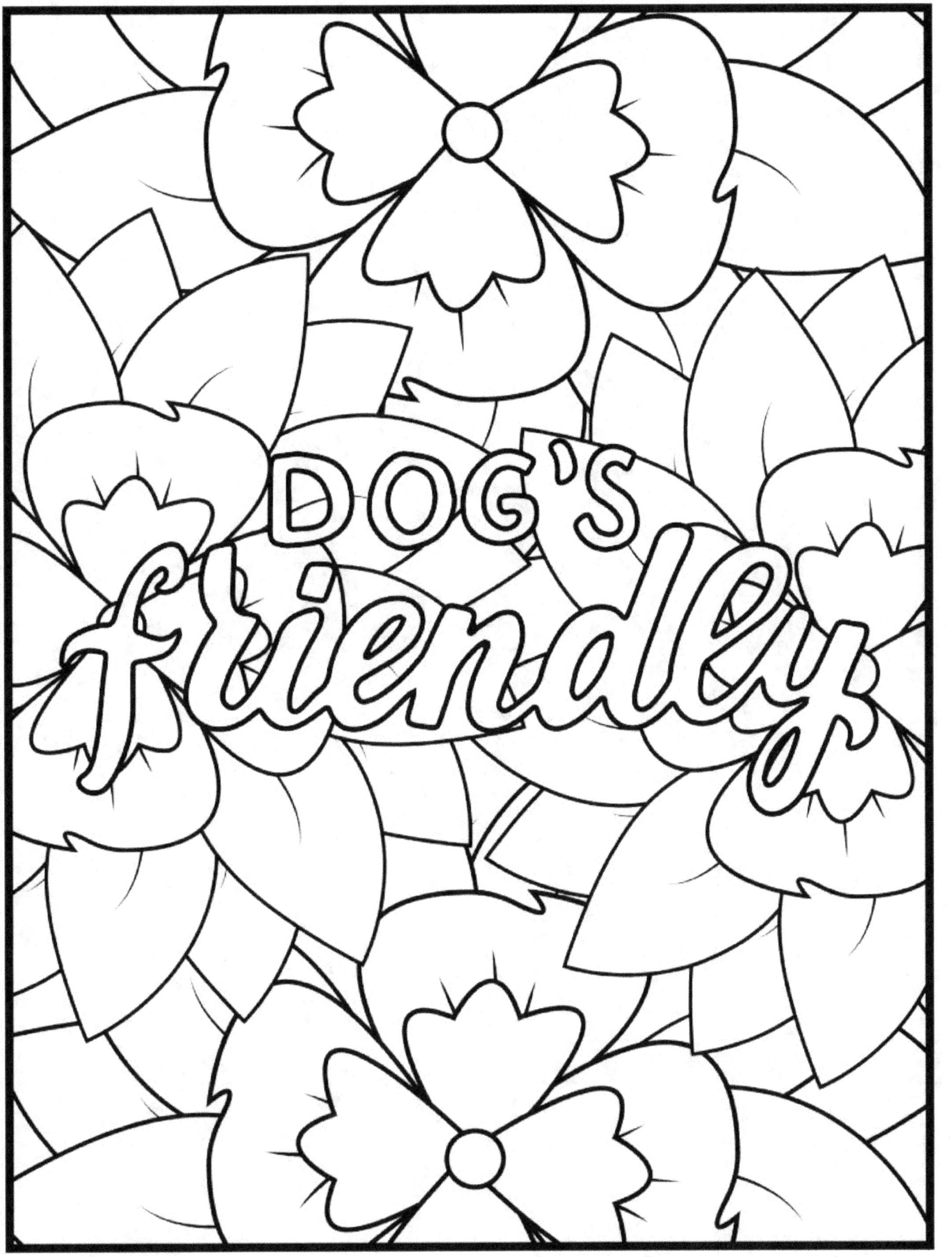
DOG'S
friendly

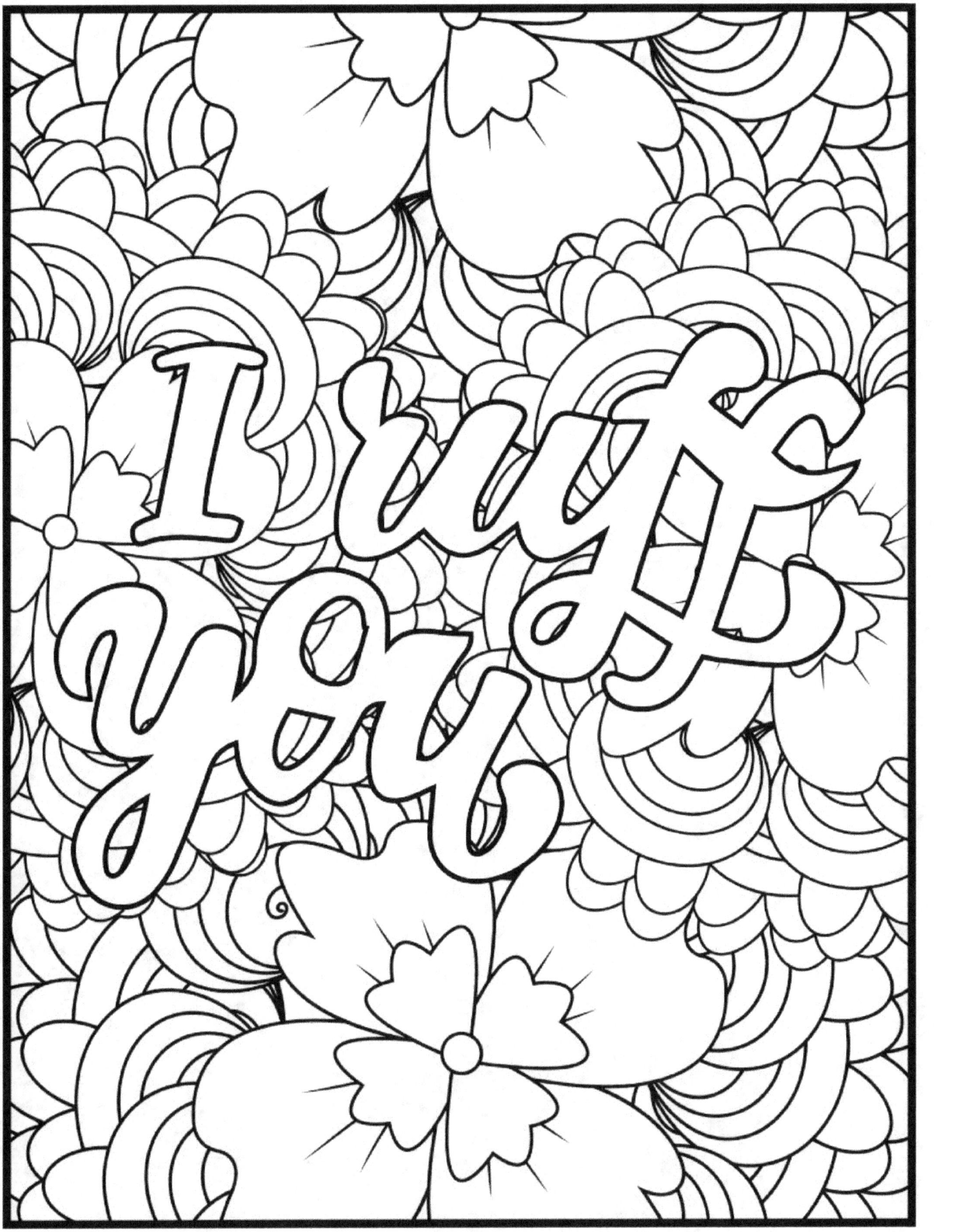
I ruff you

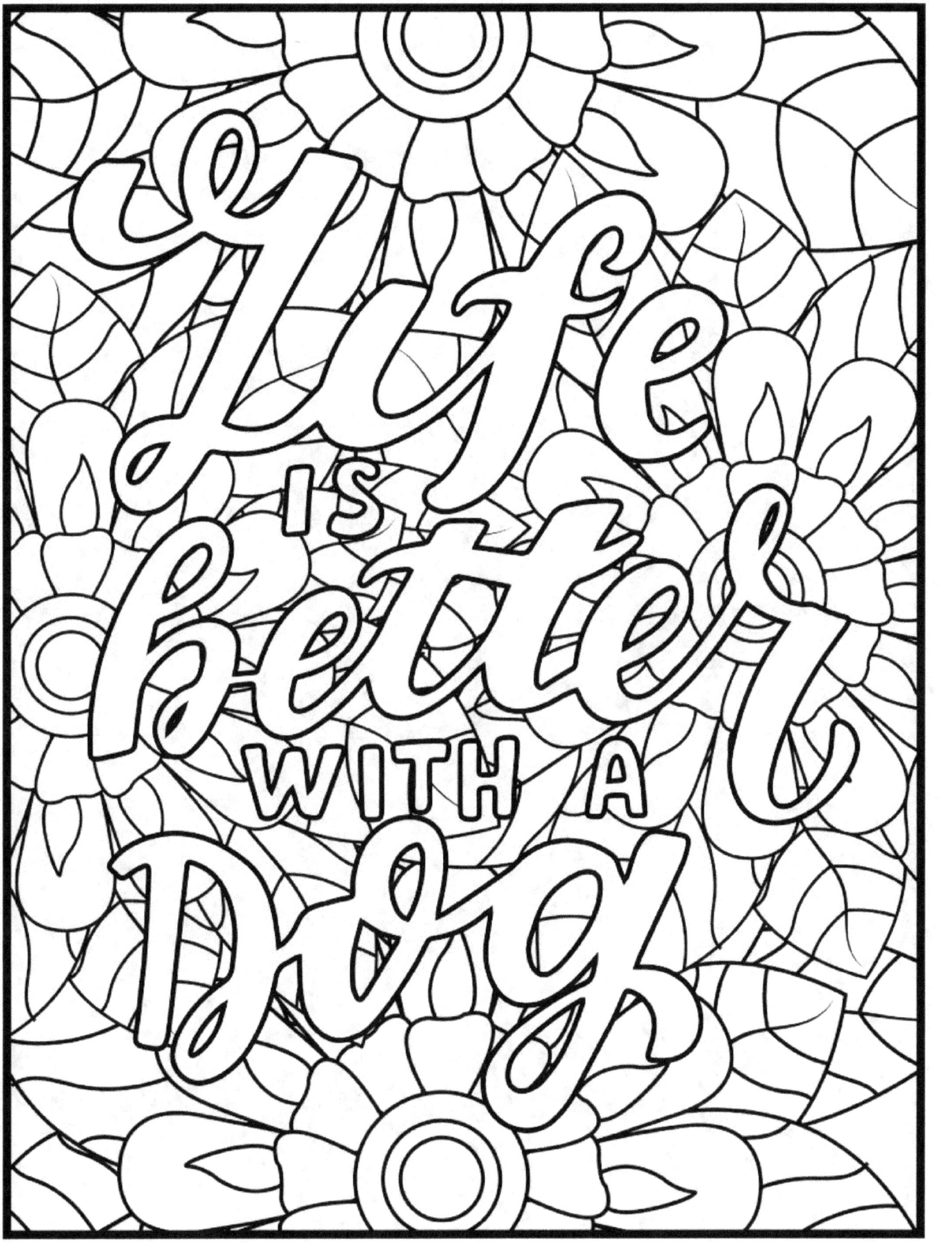
Life
IS
better
WITH A
Dog

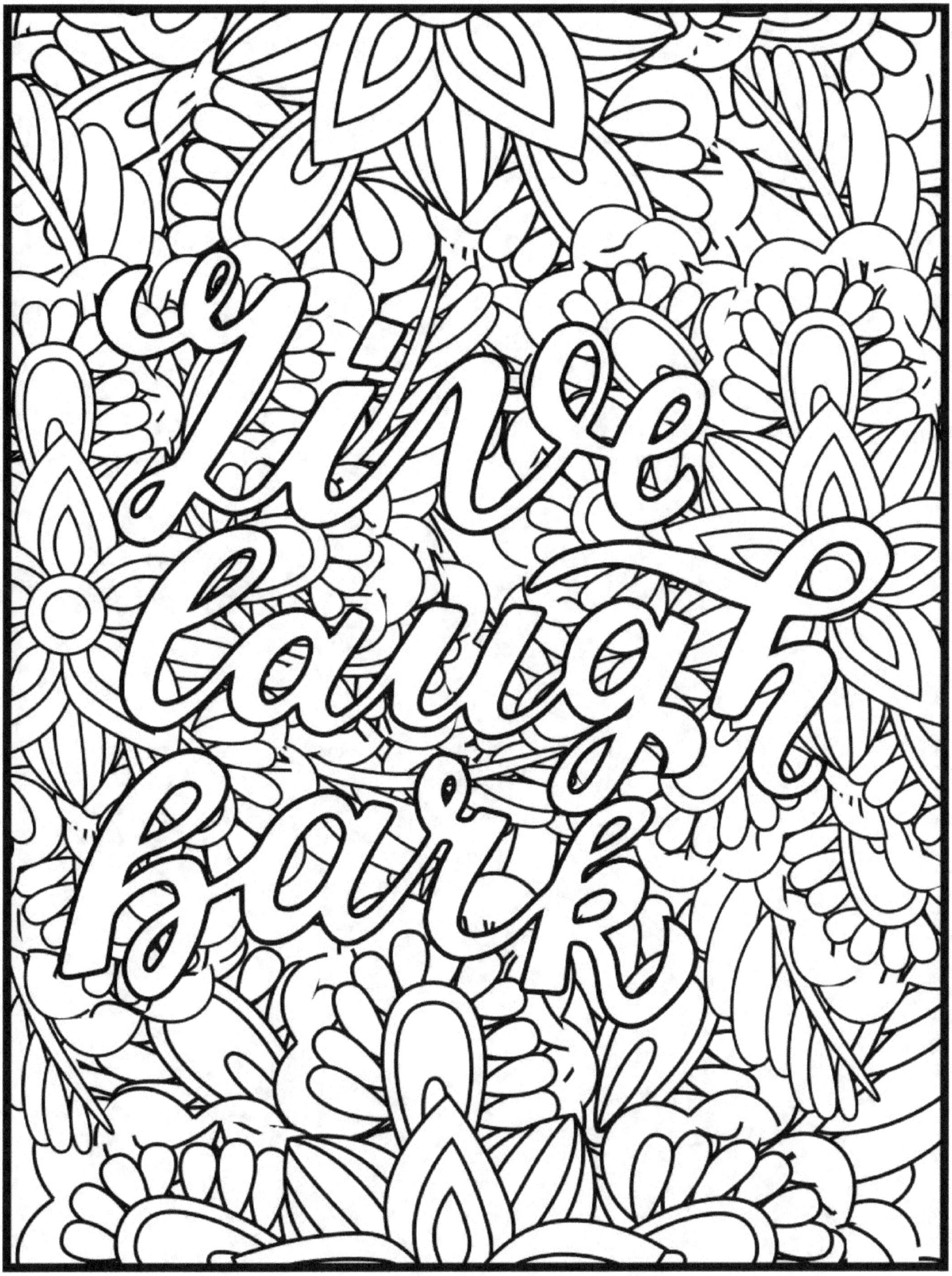
live
laugh
bark

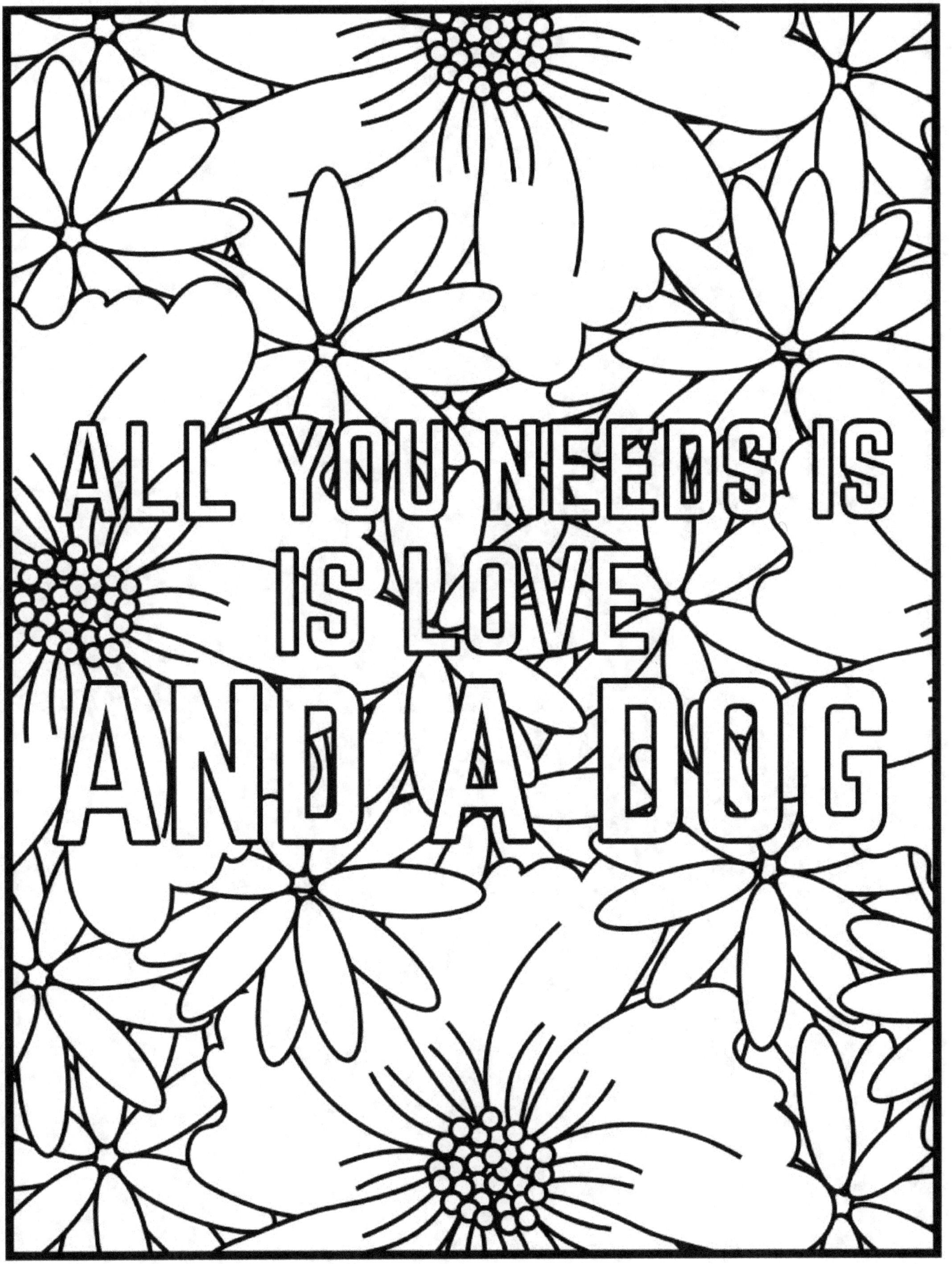
ALL YOU NEEDS IS
IS LOVE
AND A DOG

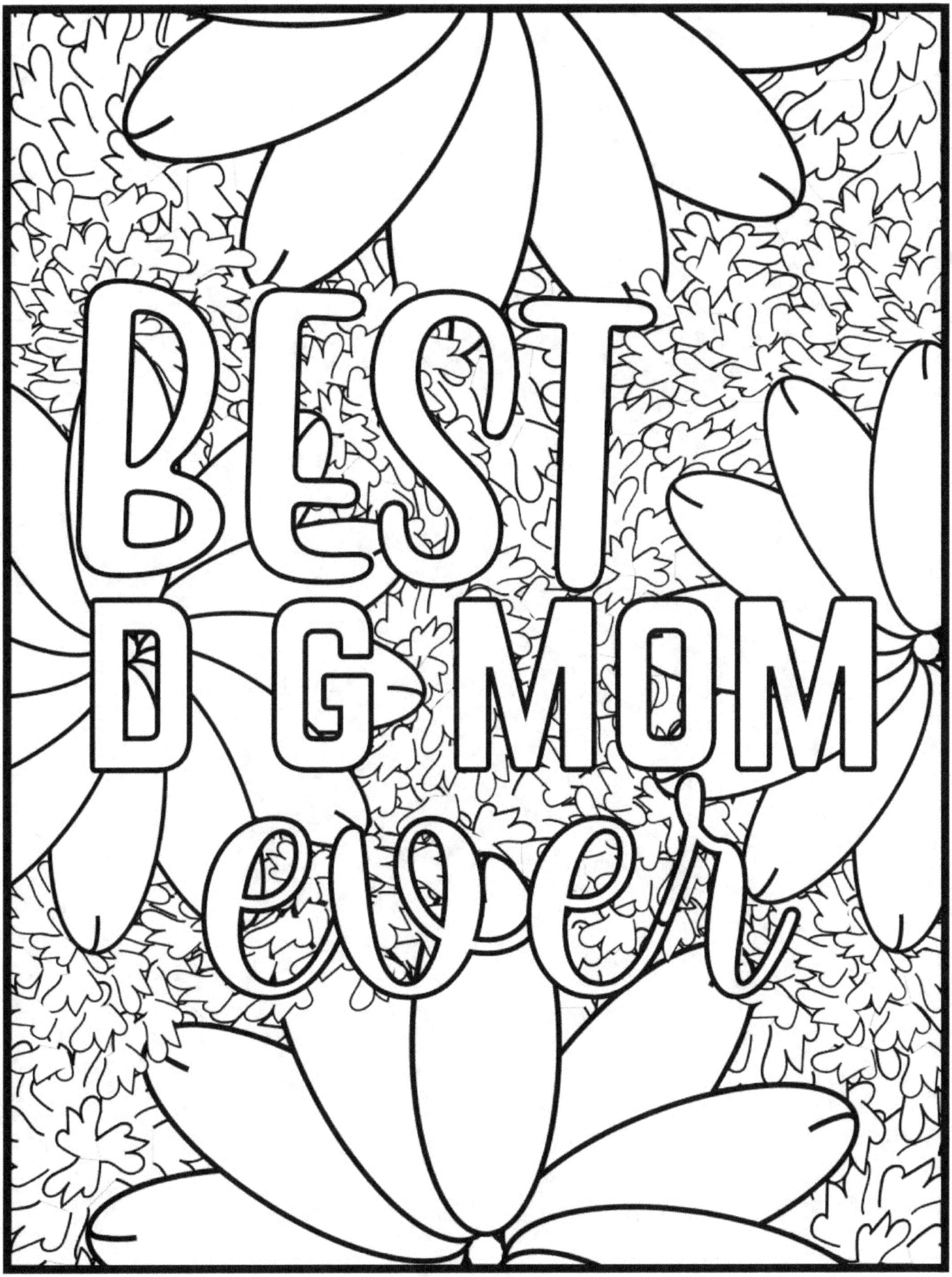
BEST
D G MOM
ever

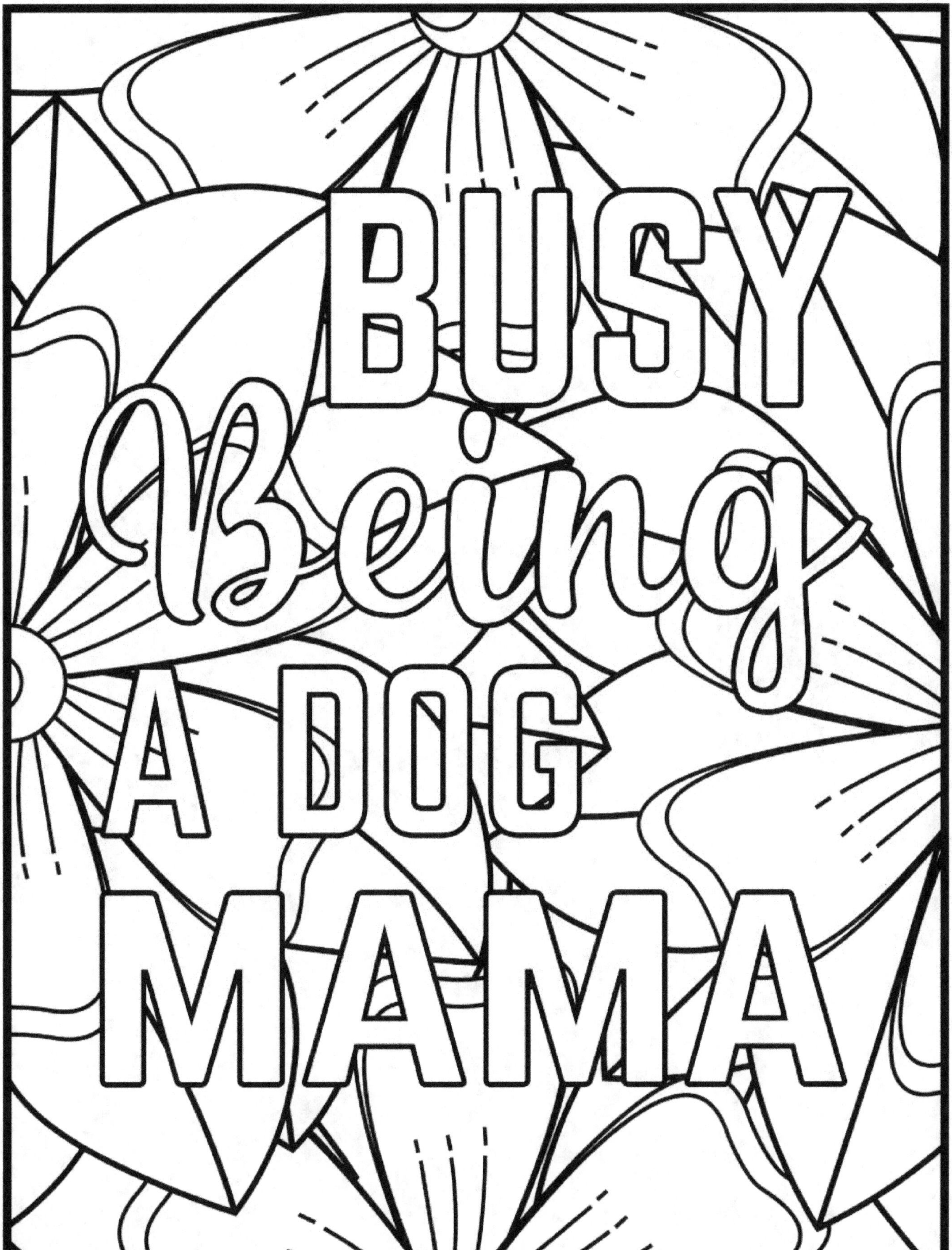
BUSY
Being
A DOG
MAMA

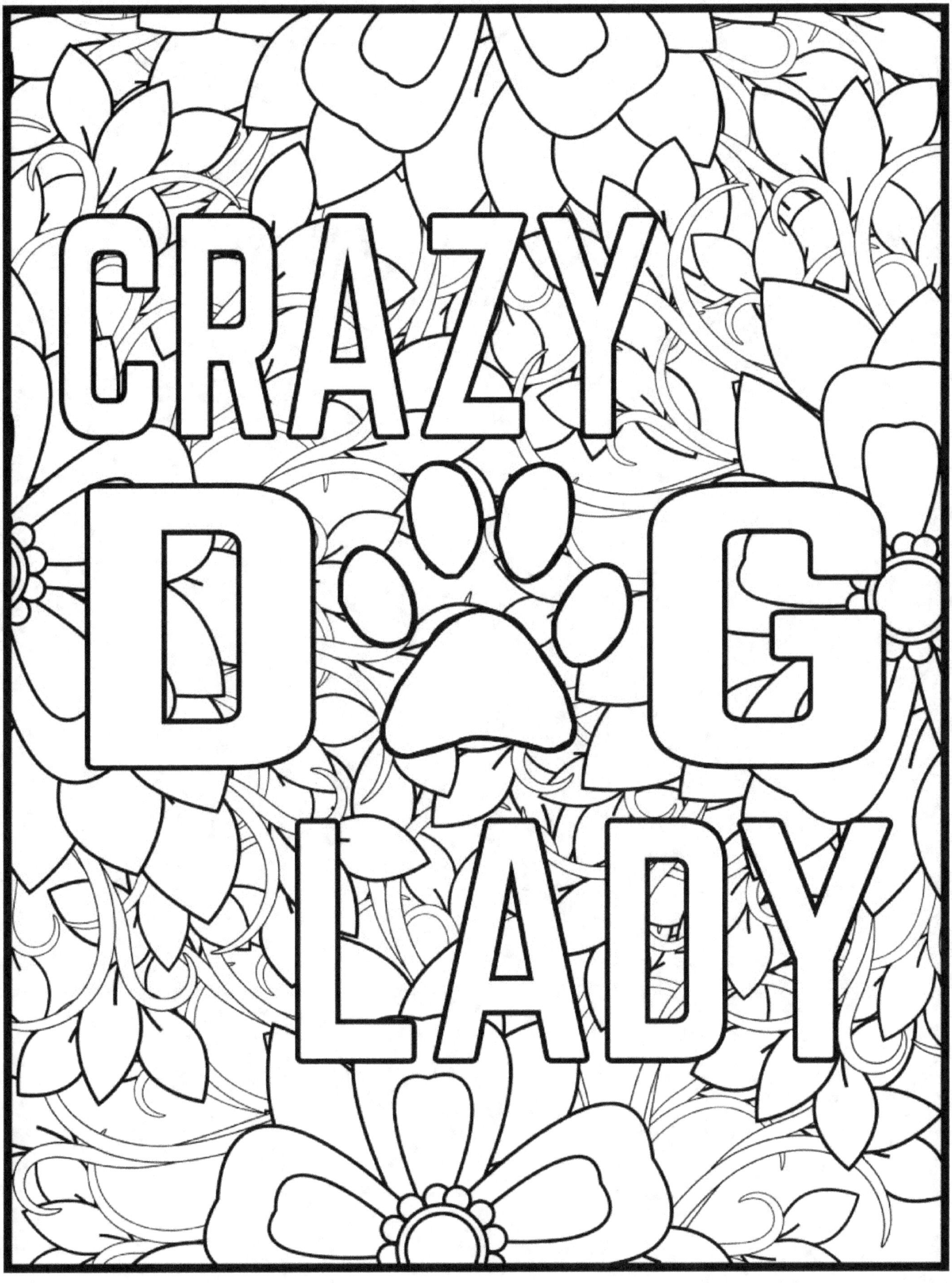
CRAZY
D G
LADY

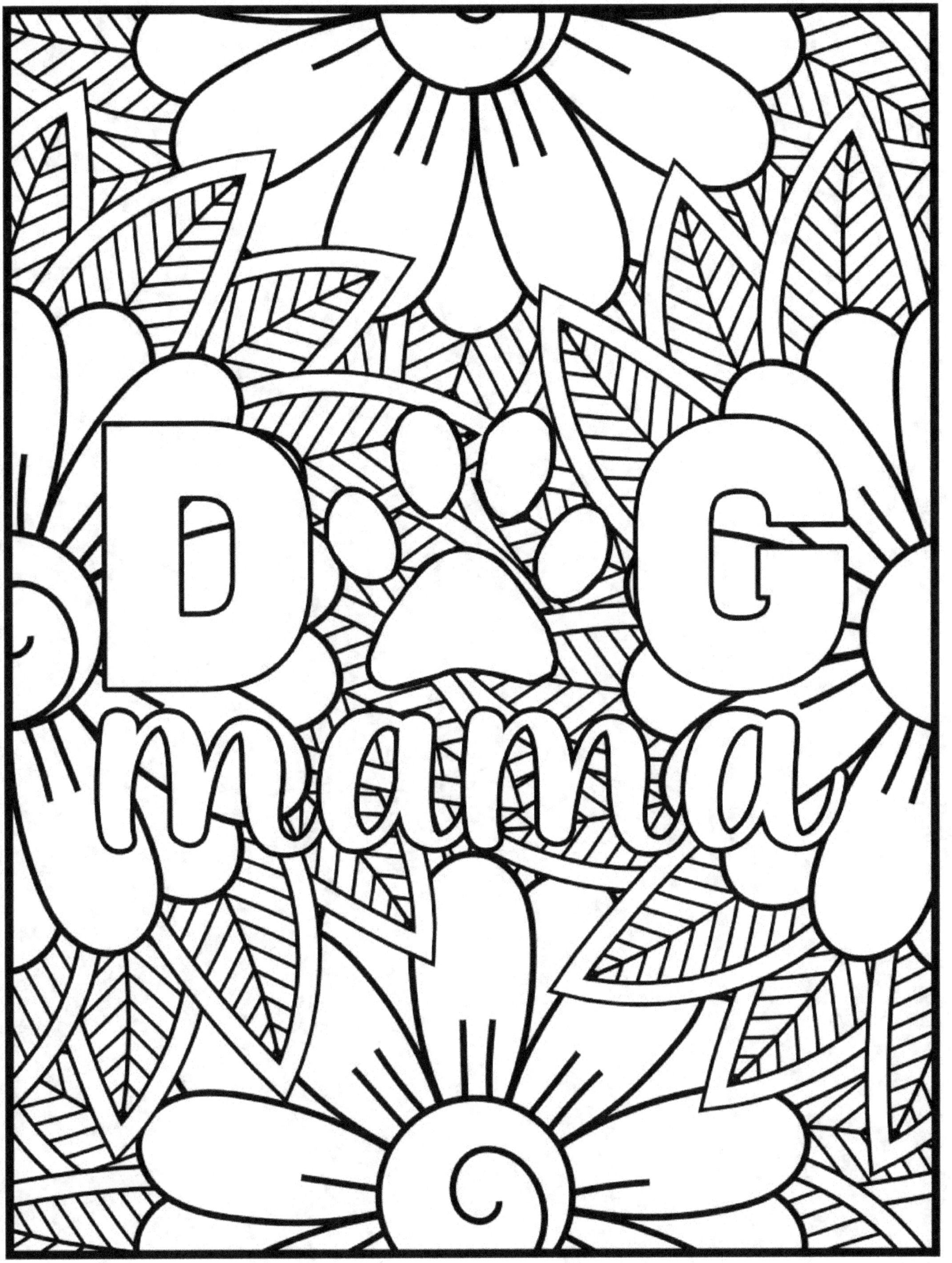
DOG
mama

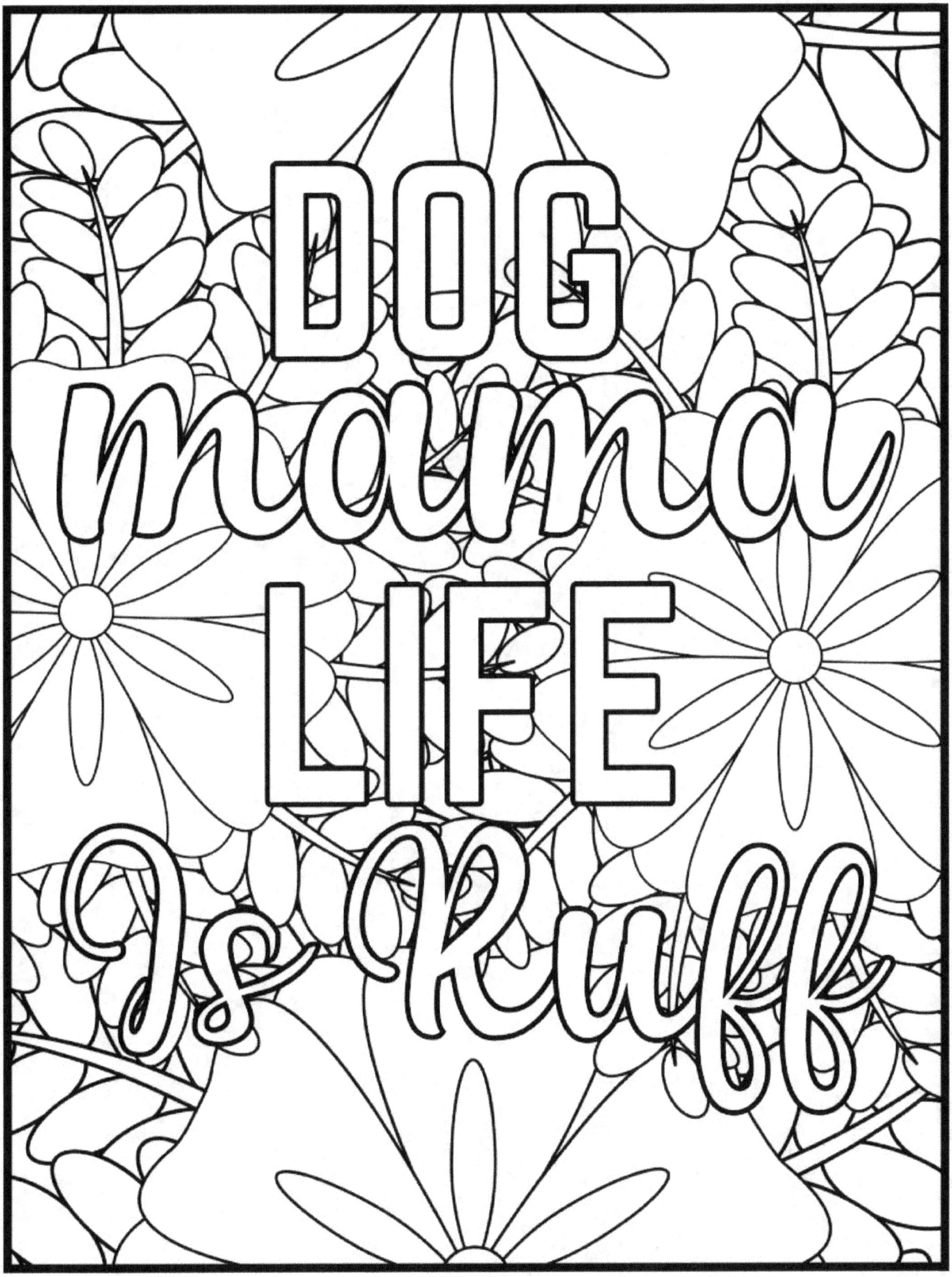
DOG
mama
LIFE
Is Ruff

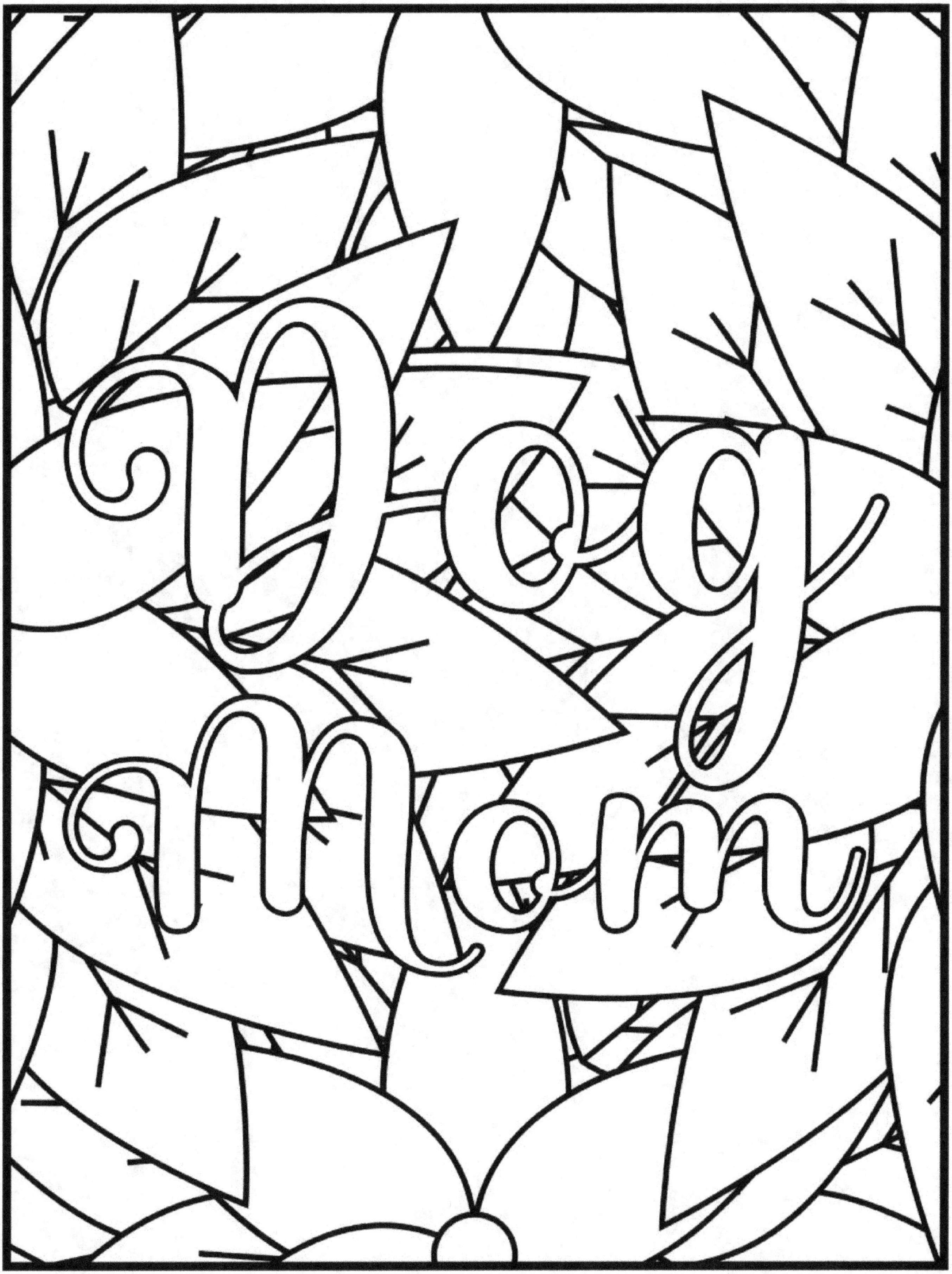
Dog
Mom

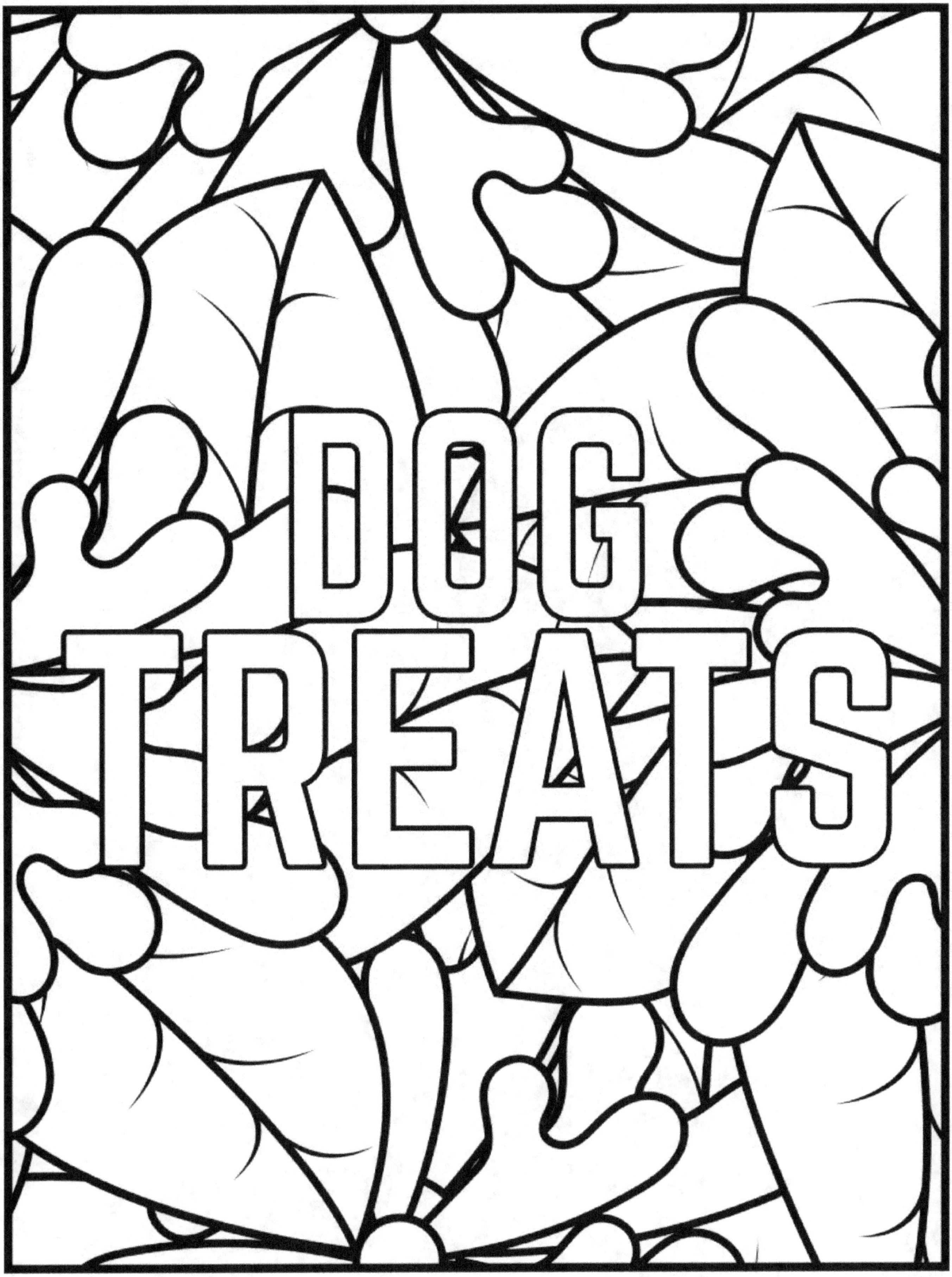
DOG
TREATS

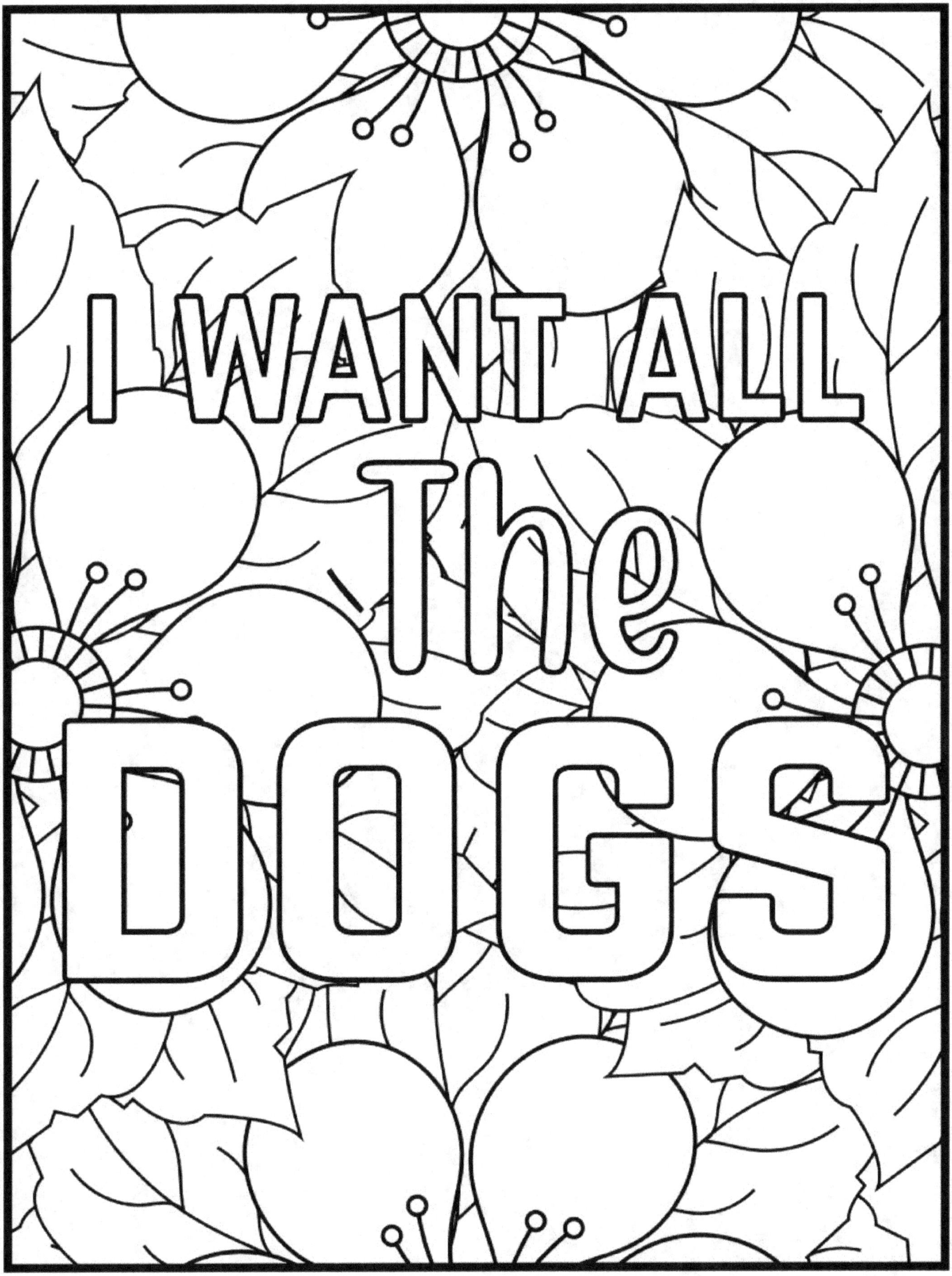
I WANT ALL
The
DOGS

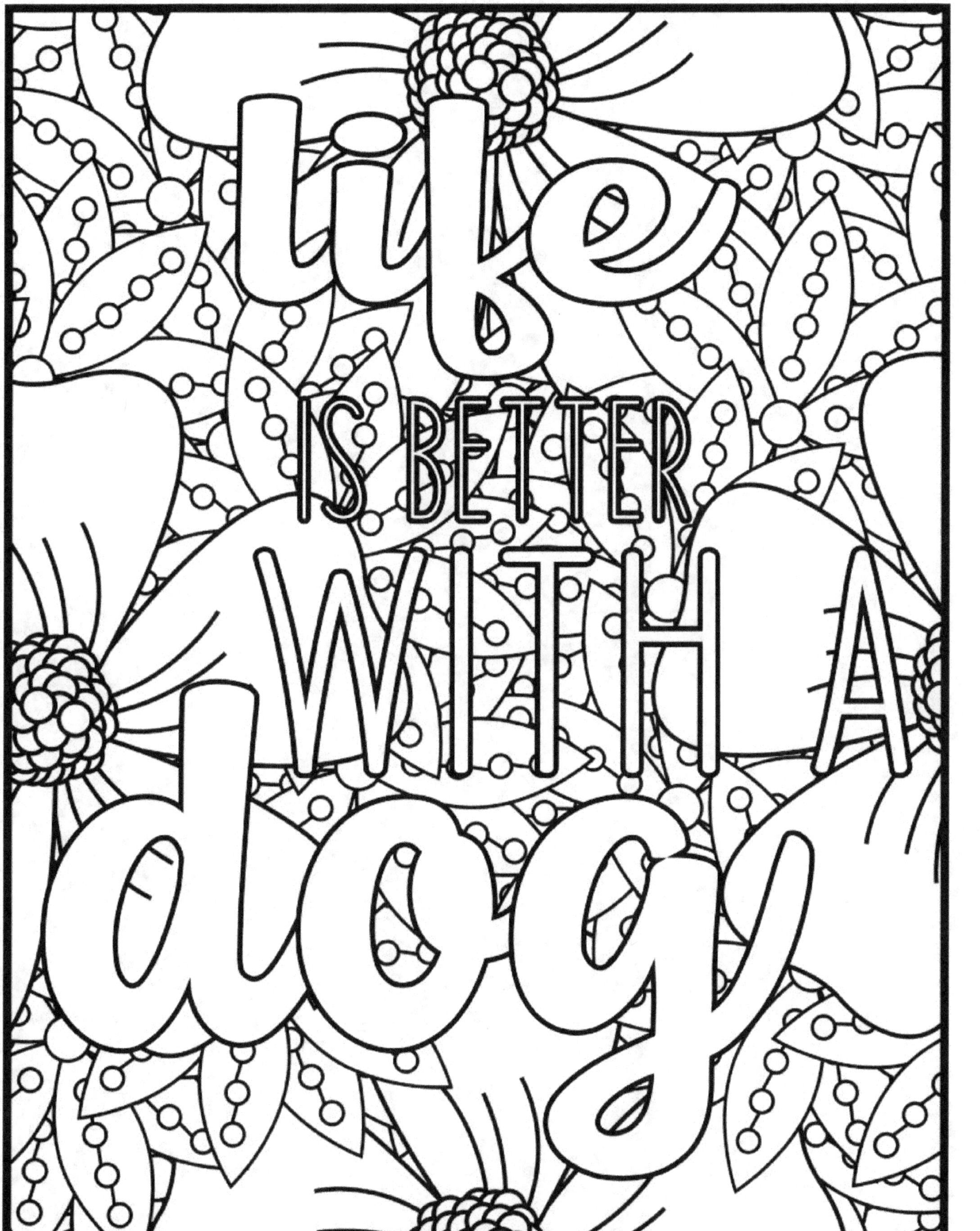
life
IS BETTER
WITH A
dog

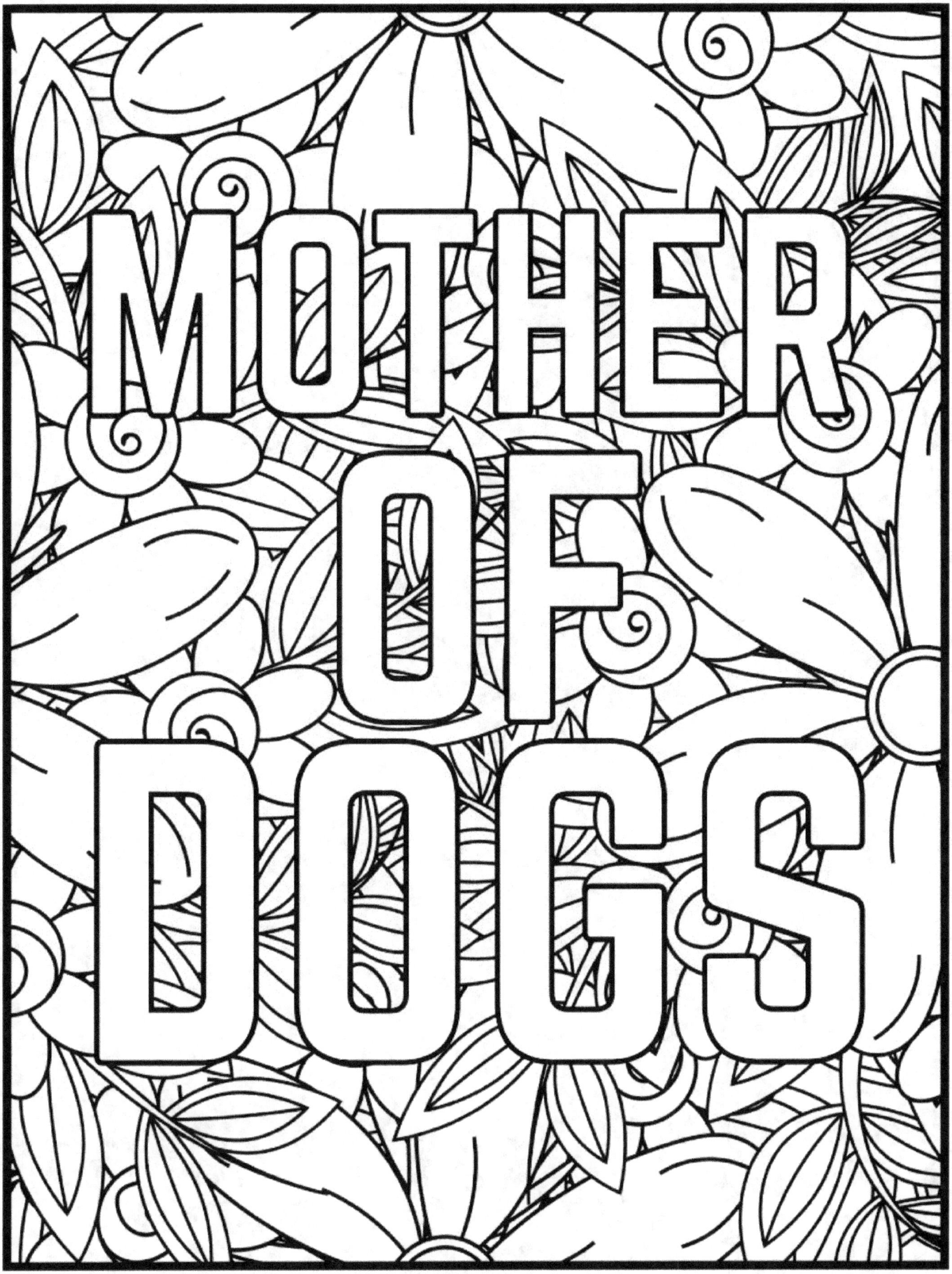
MOTHER
OF
DOGS

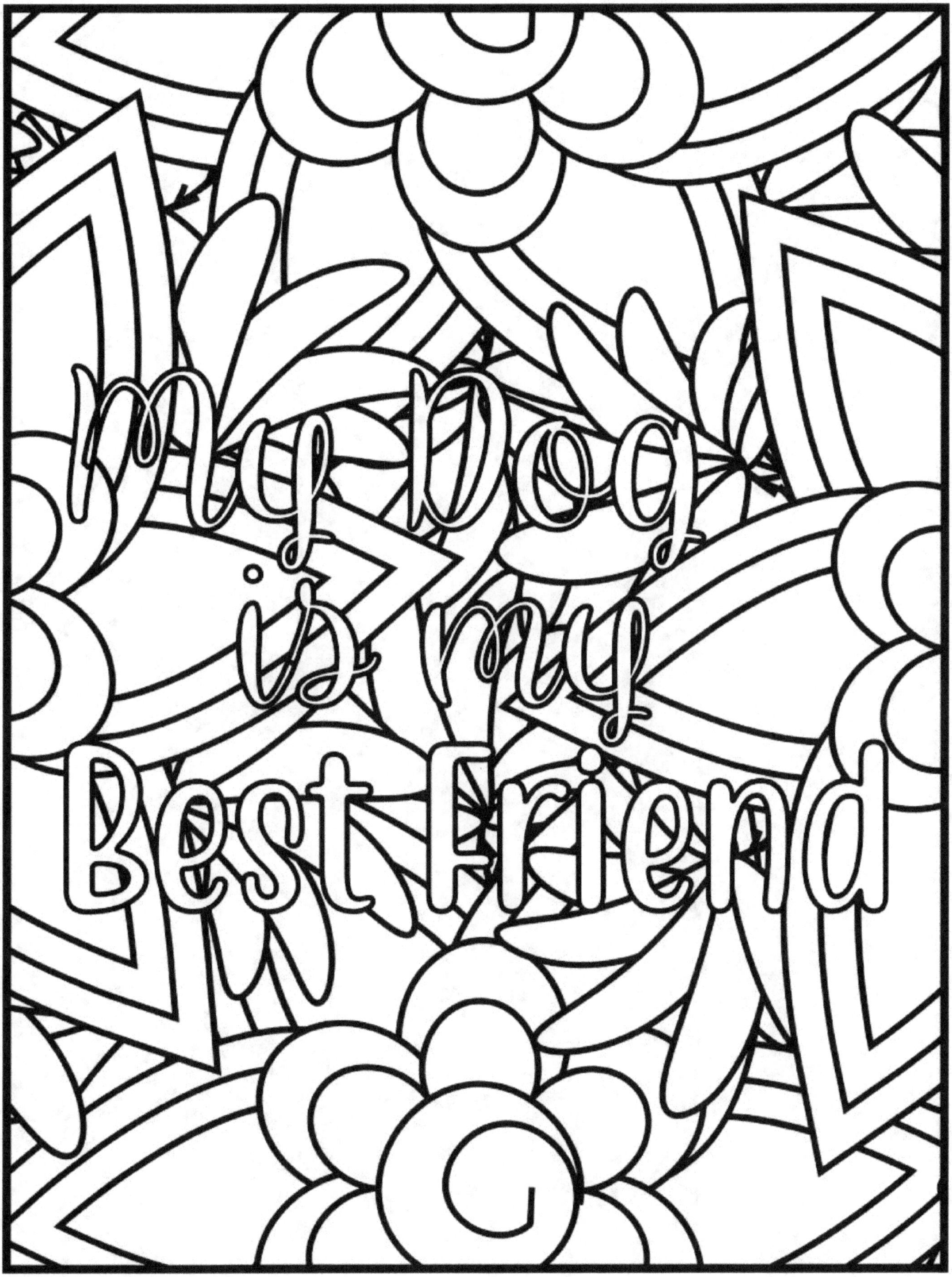
My Dog is my Best Friend

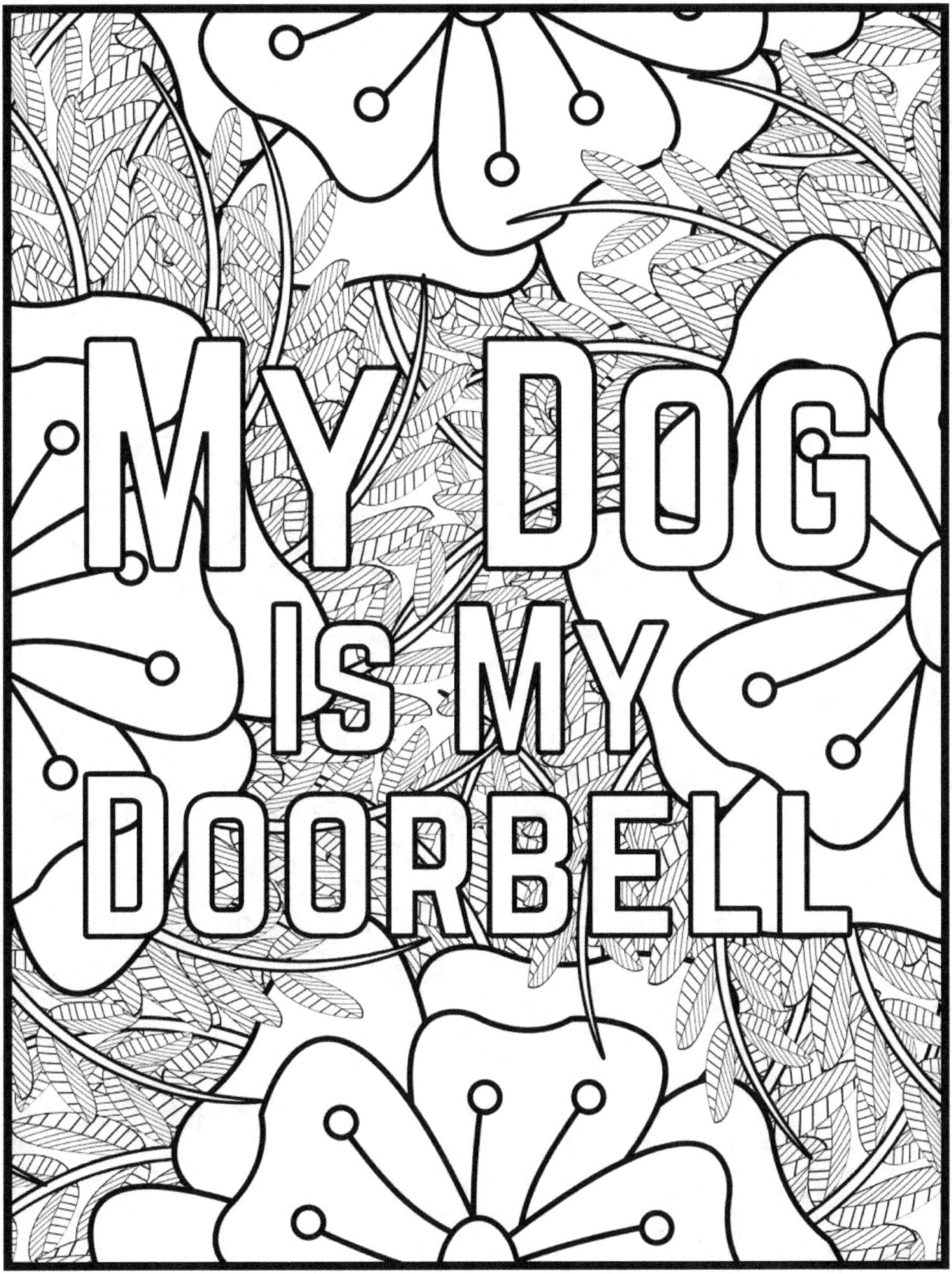
MY DOG
IS MY
DOORBELL

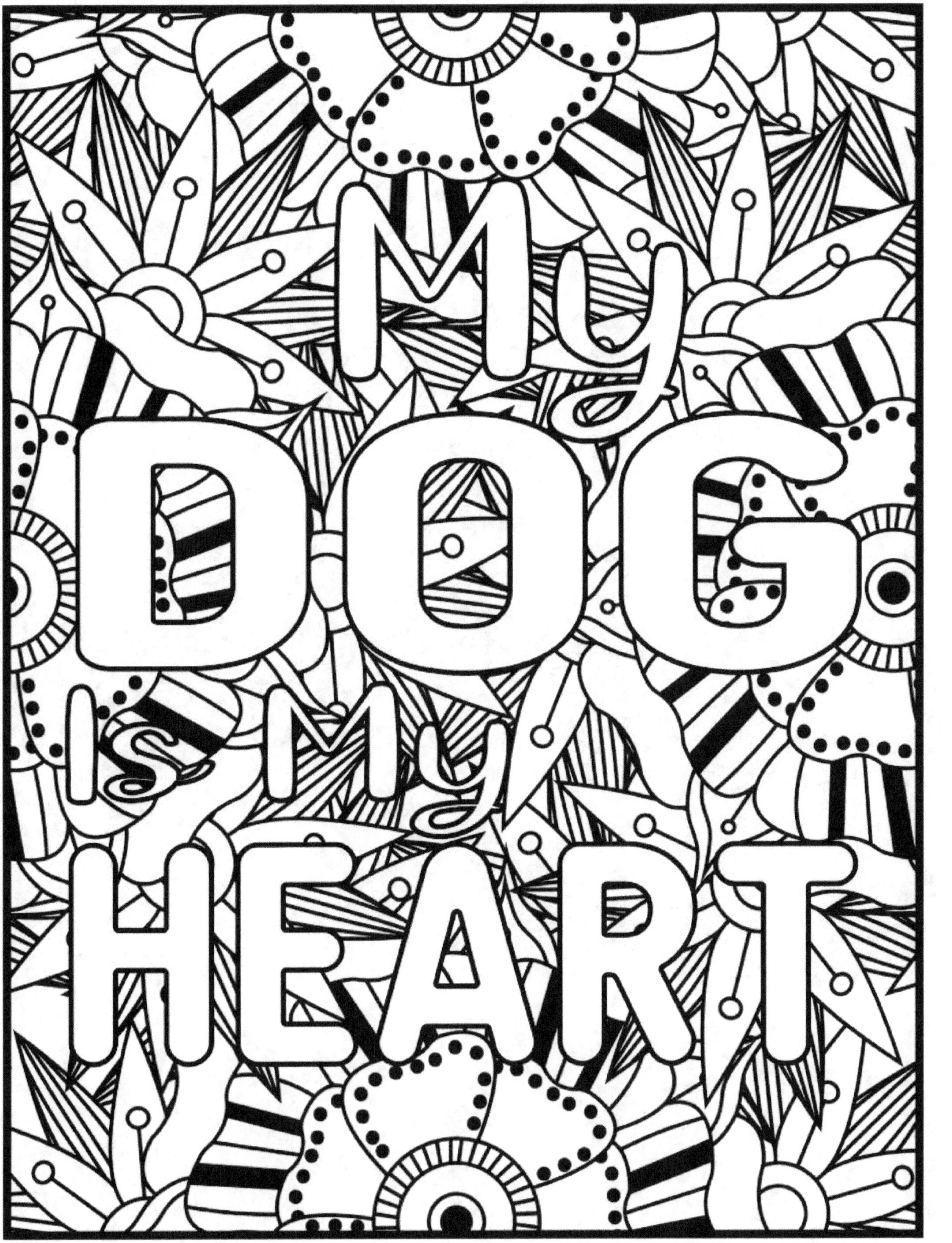
My
DOG
is My
HEART

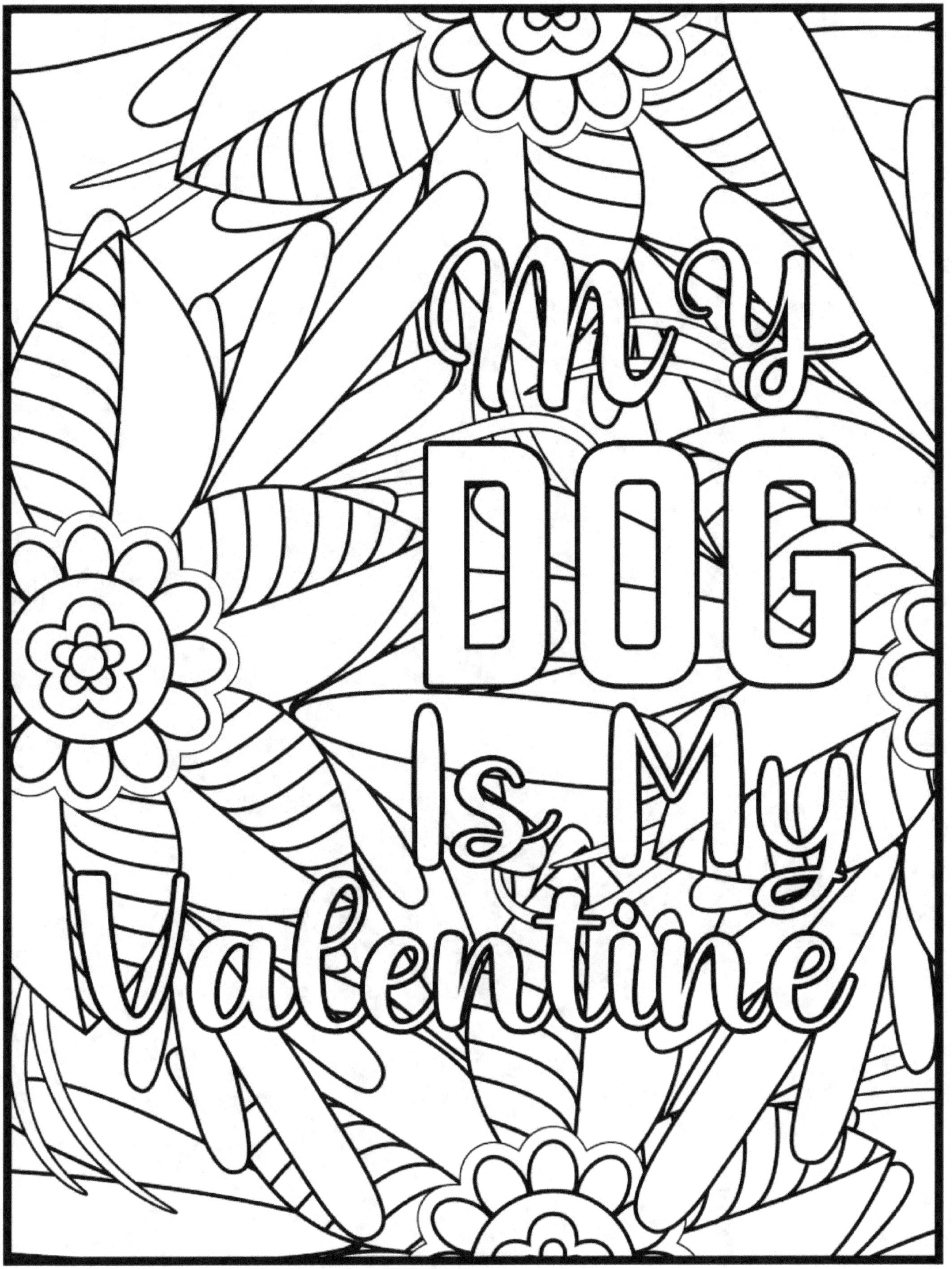
My
DOG
Is My
Valentine

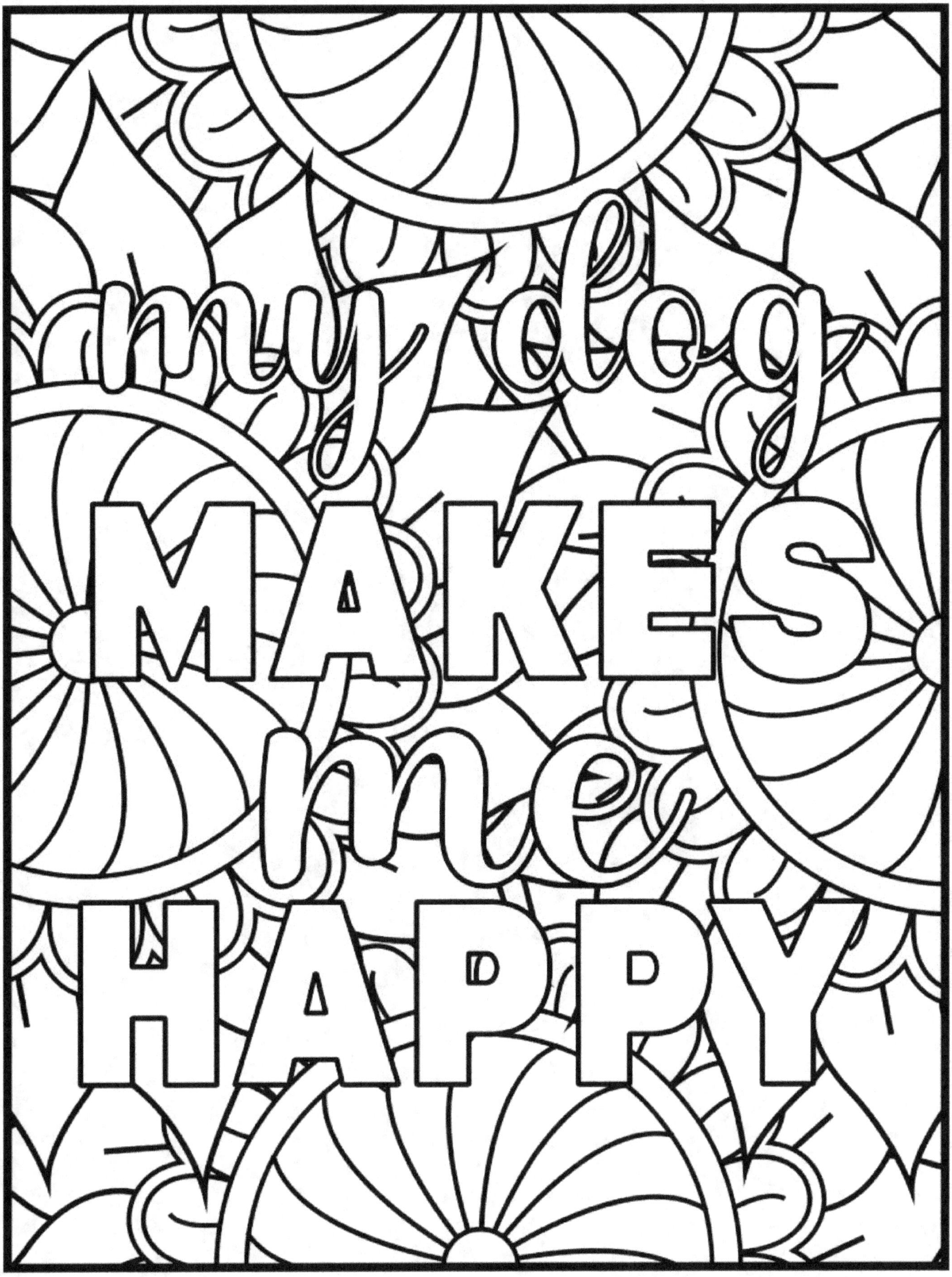
my dog
MAKES
me
HAPPY

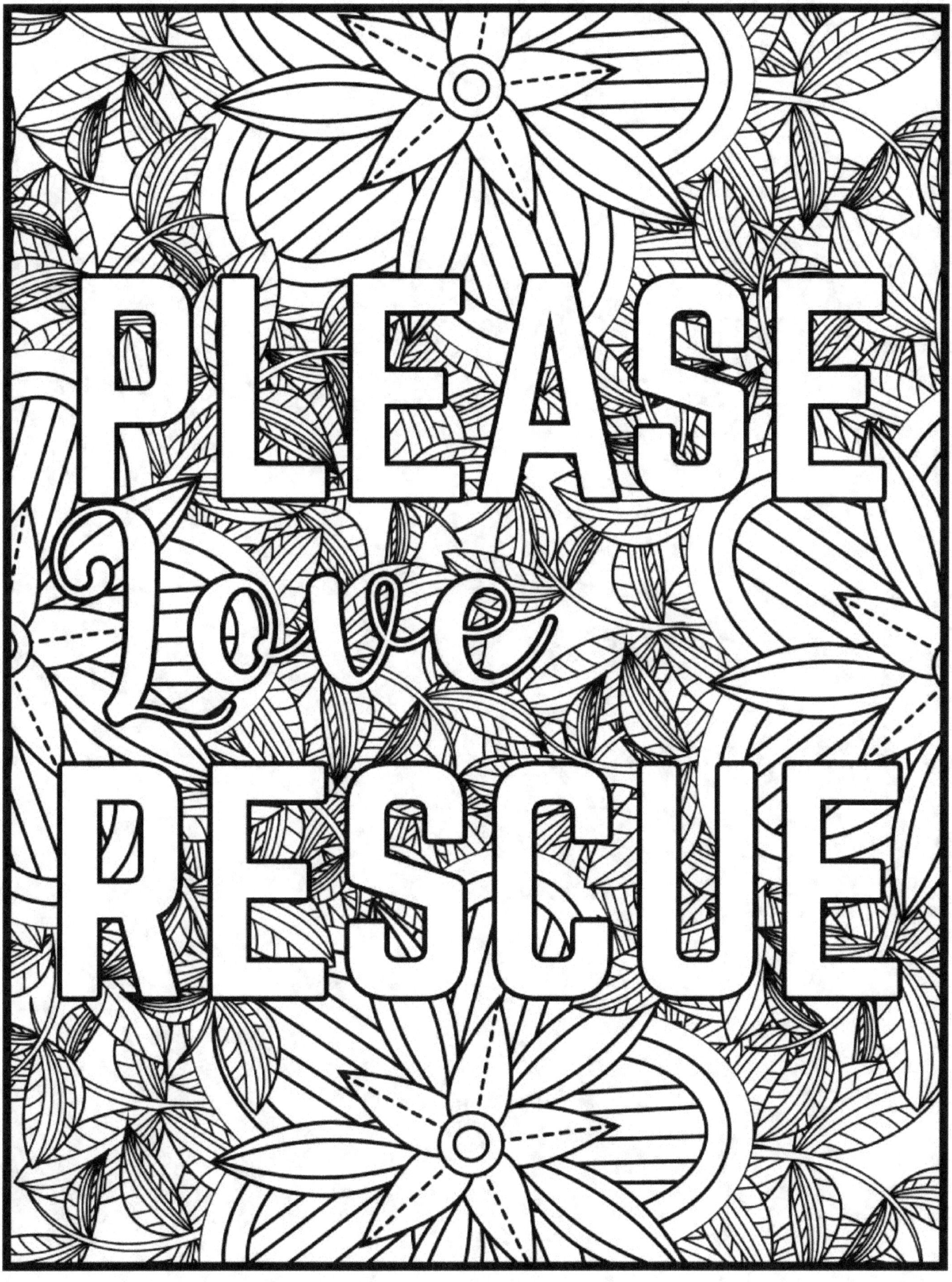
PLEASE
love
RESCUE

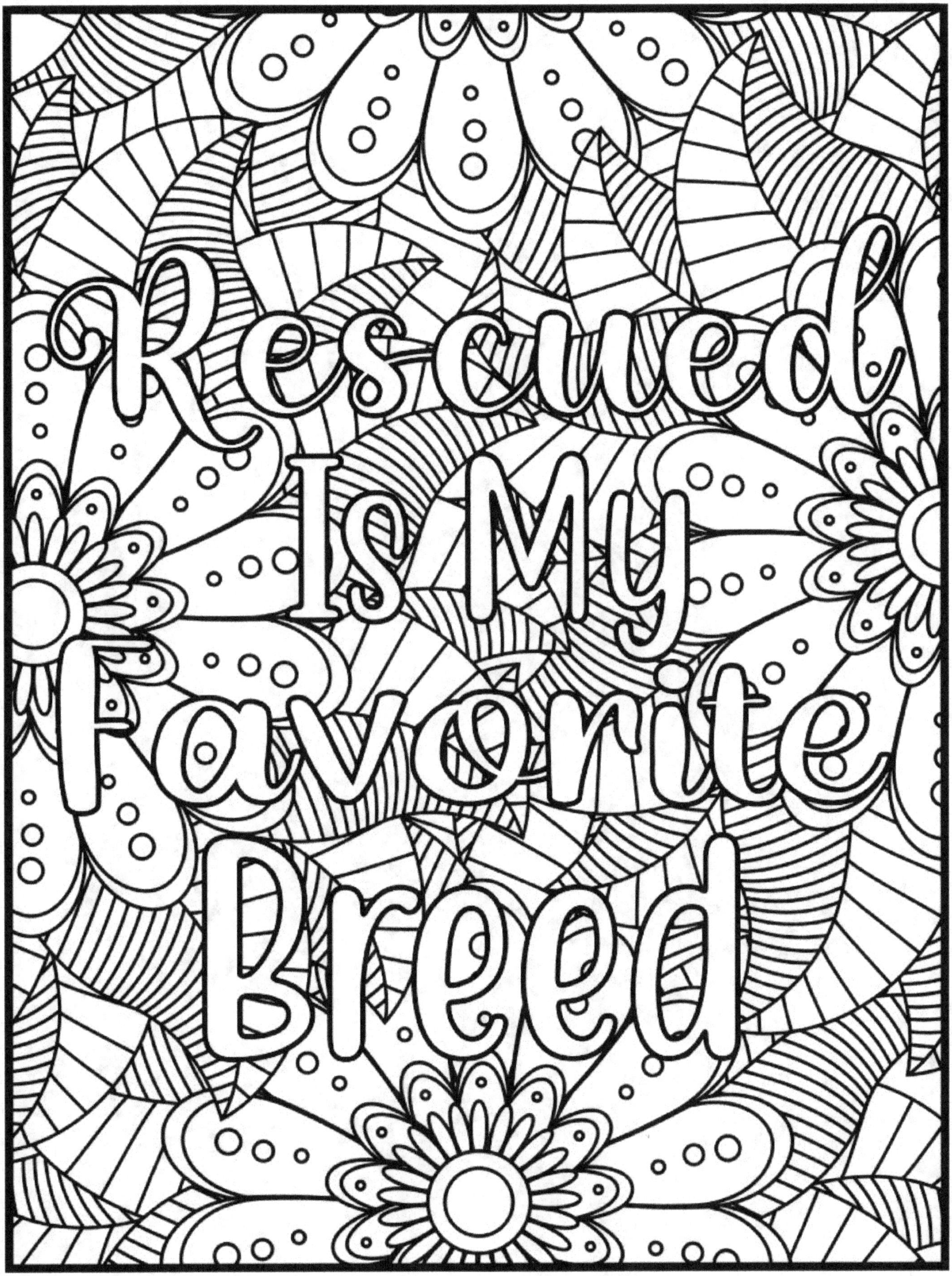
Rescued
Is My
Favorite
Breed

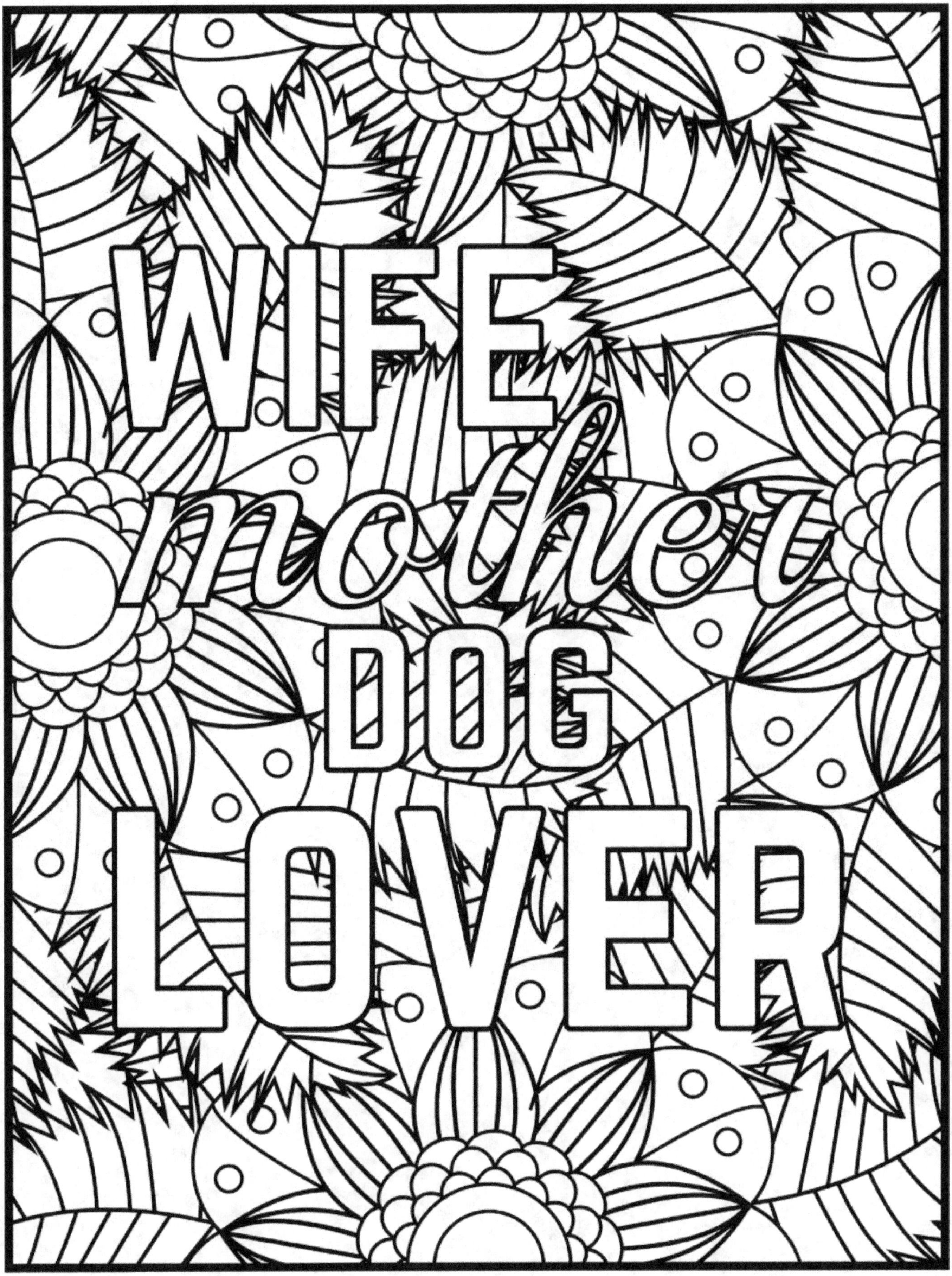
WIFE
mother
DOG
LOVER

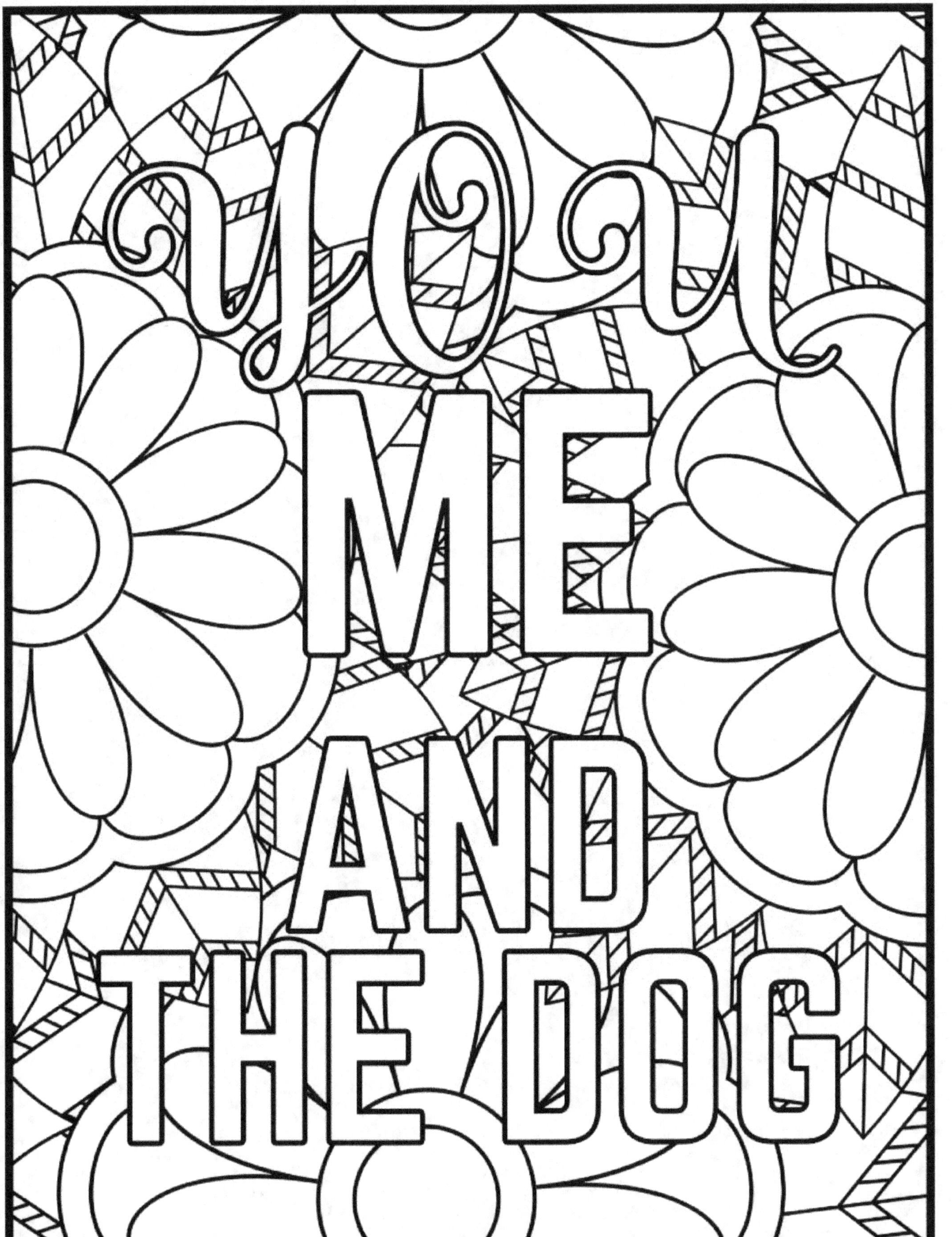
You
ME
AND
THE DOG

www.ingramcontent.com/pod-product-compliance
Lightning Source LLC
Chambersburg PA
CBHW060420220526
45465CB00008B/2953
9798822065772